DYING FOR A HOME

A LOT OF PEOPLE TALK THE TALK about Social Justice. Cathy Crowe walks the walk, and she walks it together with the most vulnerable in our society. The powerful ignore her at their peril – she can't be stopped and she can't be silenced. Thank heavens for that. Cathy shines a light on the dark little secret of poverty in our affluent country. If people like her ran our country, we'd all be better off.

    – Buzz Hargrove, President, CAW-Canada

CATHY CROWE? THERE IS NO MORE remarkable person I know in Canada. Her work has saved hundreds of lives on the streets of Toronto. Here's your opportunity to hear from some of the people she knows. Listen, Listen, Listen.

    – Shirley Douglas, actor, activist

CATHY CROWE HAS GIVEN US A GIFT – she has invited us into her life, and introduced us to her fabulous circle of friends. They are sophisticated, wise, and worldly. The only thing they have in common is that they are displaced people, discarded and dehoused by a system that has produced unprecedented wealth and prosperity, and at the same time, a permanent underclass of a quarter of a million homeless. Read this book and it will pierce the surface of your complacency, touch the core of your humanity, tickle you and teach you in equal measure. It will literally change the way you walk down the street.

    – Avi Lewis, filmmaker, journalist

DYING
for a
HOME

Homeless Activists Speak Out

CATHY CROWE

with

Nancy Baker · Brian Boyd · Bonnie and Kerre Briggs · Kevin Clarke
The Colonel · Dri · James Kagoshima · Marty Lang · Melvin Tipping

BETWEEN THE LINES
TORONTO

Dying for a Home

First published in 2007 by
Between the Lines
720 Bathurst Street, Suite #404
Toronto, Ontario M5S 2R4
Canada
1-800-718-7201
www.btlbooks.com

LIBRARY AND ARCHIVES CANADA CATALOGUING IN PUBLICATION
Crowe, Cathy, 1952–
    Dying for a home : homeless activists speak out / by Cathy Crowe ; with
Nancy Baker ... [et al.].
Includes bibliographical references.
ISBN 978-1-897071-22-9
1. Homelessness—Canada. I. Baker, Nancy II. Title.
HV4509.C76 2007   362.5'0971   C2007-900342-7

Cover and text design by David Vereschagin, Quadrat Communications

Second printing July 2007

Printed in Canada

Between the Lines gratefully acknowledges assistance for its publishing activities from the Canada Council for the Arts, the Ontario Arts Council, the Government of Ontario through the Ontario Book Publishers Tax Credit program and through the Ontario Book Initiative, and the Government of Canada through the Book Publishing Industry Development Program.

To the wind that shakes the barley

A WORD
FROM CATHY

THE CONTENTS OF MY NURSING BAG REVEAL THE HARD TRUTH of my specialty: street nursing. My patients are homeless. Many have been so for ten years or more. Canada's dirty little secret is not so secret anymore. My bandages no longer cover the wounds. My vitamins will not prevent the white plague of tuberculosis from taking another life. Duct tape to fix a cardboard shelter, or a bus ticket to get an elderly man to a hot air grate, will not ensure a peaceful night of safety and sleep. Only a roof will do that, and I am not a carpenter.

Over the years a number of people had asked me to write a book about myself and my work as a street nurse. The idea had never appealed to me. Eventually, my friend Morris Wolfe – a writer who excels in giving other people a voice through his own writing – urged me to do the same. After all, since I already got so much attention, why not give homeless people – the reason I'm a street nurse – a chance to tell their own stories?

This made a lot of sense to me. I felt that there were heros and heroines in the movement who deserved the kind of attention frequently focused on me.

The selection process was simple. I picked people I had known and worked with for a long time: homeless people who had been activists, speaking out on the issues and speaking out for the solutions. They also had to be people with whom I had a close, personal connection.

I worried that people would be nervous or mistrustful, in particular because of the treatment some of them had received in Shaughnessy Bishop-Stall's 2004 book *Down to This: Squalor and Splendour in a Big-City Shantytown*. But they agreed, and accepted the invitation with enthusiasm and pride. I felt trusted.

In the summer of 2004 I began interviewing people with Morris's assistance, using a simple tape recorder. I was a novice and my nervousness showed.

I was teased. With time, a more natural rhythm established itself, and I carried on alone. Interviews took place in parks, on park benches, and frequently in restaurants and donut shops. It didn't take long before I began to get eager calls asking, "When is our next interview?" especially when there were new developments in people's lives.

Two of the people I profiled had, in fact, died (and, tragically, another has died since – see the Epilogue), but their stories are so important that I pieced them together, drawing on film footage, their own writings, and television news clips.

By the fall of 2005 I had finished the bulk of the story collecting and the process of transcribing hours of interviews. I was accepted for a residency at the Blue Mountain Centre in the Adirondacks to put the book together. I was the only non-American in the group. At the last minute I threw all the interview tapes into my carry-on luggage. Thank goodness I did. The whole time I was away I was so homesick for Canada and for these friends. I would often walk or hike with my headset on, listening again to their voices. I remember hearing Dri talking about being in the bush up north, while I was in a similar place hiking through the woods. Some of the tapes made me laugh. Many made me cry.

Each person has had the chance to see, to add to, and to edit, their own story. Proceeds from this book will be shared equally among these activists.

□ □ □

My experience as a street nurse since 1989 has convinced me that the best way to end homelessness is with a national housing program. Housing is a basic building block for a healthy society – it's as important as our national health program.

The real experts – the homeless activists – explain why:

MELVIN TIPPING, EXPERT WITNESS

Melvin articulates his experience of the street with underpinnings of political analysis. His eloquence and passion for politics and current affairs have made him a natural spokesperson. He was the only person with personal experience of homelessness who was allowed status as an expert witness at the 1996 Freezing Deaths Inquest.

DRI, URBAN LEGEND

Welder, miner, prospector, explosives expert, cement mason, union rep, artist, secret cameraman, poet, Tent City squatter, great dancer, son, father, political activist. Urban legend.

NANCY BAKER, WITNESS TO IT ALL

Just because she's housed now doesn't stop her from reminding politicians that there are too many homeless people still out there. Nancy was the first woman to move into Toronto's Tent City waterfront squatter camp. She's gutsy. She's lost more people than anyone I know, and she's still fighting. She regularly reminds me to chastise politicians: "Tell them that we're dying!"

MARTY LANG, TENT CITY LEADER

I've known Marty more than twenty years. He's soft-spoken, smart and reliable. He's kind. He's a tease. He was one of the quiet leaders at Tent City, staying out of the limelight. Today, he speaks to national and international housing and homeless experts. He shrugs off the experience. After all, he's the expert.

BRIAN BOYD, THE BOY NEXT DOOR

Brian – "the boy next door" from Northern Ontario. Handsome, athletic, fun, good with all things electronic. He was a DJ on his hometown radio station. Homeless, he became one of the most articulate speakers on the issue. Almost everyone says you can't talk about Brian without talking about the Colonel, Brian's "street brother."

THE COLONEL, TOWN CRIER

The Colonel, as his name suggests, is a bit of a character. Far from his hometown in Prince Edward Island, and a career in the army as an air traffic controller, the Colonel now fights homelessness. He loves a microphone, even though he doesn't need one.

JAMES KAGOSHIMA, WISE GUIDE

James was my eyes, ears, and voice on the street. He knew the grates, the sidewalks, the shelters. He went to places I couldn't always go, and was persistent in the message to his "street friends" that they must join in the fight for better shelter conditions and for housing. More than anyone, he made me realize how tenuous life is.

KEVIN CLARKE, STREET POLITICIAN

A consummate politician, Kevin spreads the faith that each person is a treasure, worthy of respect, love, and housing. Kevin literally tries to curb homelessness from the curb by changing attitudes and talking about human rights: the right to respect, the right to housing. His favourite place to deliver his message is Bay Street, the financial corridor of Canada.

BONNIE AND KERRE BRIGGS, TALENTED DUO

The ongoing adventures of Bonnie and Kerre include not only battling poverty most of their lives, but also pursuing their many hobbies and interests. They are an accomplished duo, in both their talents, and their perseverance. They write, act, perform, and battle. They are devoted to fighting for the underdog and challenging myths about homelessness and poverty.

DYING FOR A HOME

CHAPTER 1

CATHY CROWE

STREET NURSE

Cathy celebrating opening of emergency shelter at Fort York Armoury, 2004

PICTURE A REFUGEE CAMP:

A quarter of a million people. Ten thousand are children. There is no more room. Some people will do anything to avoid entering. Tens of thousands stay with family or friends. Another two thousand sleep rough – in cars, on grates, in parks, by riverbeds, under bridges, in the woods. Some are squatting in empty buildings and old factories, or building shantytowns and tent cities. They sometimes remain there for years, enduring the cold, harsh Canadian winters.

Back in the camp, conditions are substandard. Common areas are filled with mats to accommodate extra people in the winter months. In some sections there are only two toilets for more than a hundred people. Staffing is inadequate and violence is rampant. Entire sections are staffed only by volunteers. One of them discovered a man dead in his sleeping bag on a recent morning.

Diseases and outbreaks consistent with overcrowding are the norm. The tuberculosis infection rate is four times higher than in the population not hit by the disaster. Other infections – diarrhea, colds, and flus – are rampant. During a recent outbreak of Norwalk virus, a police lockdown in part of the camp was necessary to confine healthy people who panicked and wanted out. Meanwhile, medics provided intravenous rehydration to the sick on site rather than transporting them to hospital. Bedbugs, scabies, and lice are a growing public health concern. There is even a shower room set up specifically for delousing. But for the regular shower room there's a waiting list.

Some women are pregnant. Most of the children are very young. The long-term impact on them will be profound. There are people with cancer, with multiple sclerosis, with Parkinson's, and diabetes. The death rate is also four times higher in the camp than outside, and each week people die. Occasionally someone is taken to hospital and dies there. People have been stuck in the camp for so long now that palliative care units have been set up.

Cathy with her mom and grandfather, Cobourg, 1953

Outside the camp, a government sign in a bus shelter reads: "There is help available for the homeless. A warm bed, a kind voice, a helping hand." The sign is defaced by graffiti: "Kill the homeless!" Anger and hate towards the homeless has been growing. A refugee left the camp recently and was brutally murdered – beaten in his sleeping bag in a park.

By now you've probably figured out that I am referring to the desperate situation of displaced persons – commonly known as "the homeless" – here in Canada. This refugee camp scenario describes the raw reality. The information was taken from official reports on ten of Canada's largest cities, and from my first-hand experience and work as a street nurse in Canada.

I used to call this our dirty little secret, but it's not so secret anymore, is it? This is the Canadian experience that tourist guides and history books don't mention. I ask myself, how did we let this happen? How did I end up working in refugee camp conditions in a rich country like Canada?

I grew up during the 1950s and 1960s in Cobourg, a small town nestled on Lake Ontario. My family lived in a relatively new subdivision. All around us woods were being cut down, gravel trucked in to build new streets, and houses were going up in all directions. Each day around 5 P.M. when the workmen were gone, my friends and I used to sneak into the shells of houses to play. When I was alone I spent a lot of time playing with a makeshift dollhouse made out of an empty cardboard box. We had many in our basement – my dad was Mr. Christie, a sales rep for Christie cookies. With a little bit of imagination (and lots of cookies to help), and some crayons and magazine clippings, I transformed it into a spectacular dollhouse. It was a split-level with four bedrooms, just like the one I lived in with my three younger brothers. It had furniture and crayoned walls where imaginary people lived busy lives. Maybe because home is so central to who we are, playing house has always been a popular pastime for kids. Today, my niece Alexa has the most beautiful cardboard house in her basement. Like her, I not only imagined, I believed that when everyone grew up they would have a place called home.

Alexa's cardboard dollhouse, 2006

I am a nurse. I knew from the age of five that I wanted to be a nurse. Why? Certainly one reason was that I saw my mother going off to work in her crisp, white nursing uniform and cape, and I sensed that to be a nurse would be rewarding. Also, the career choices for a girl in the fifties seemed to be either nursing or teaching, and I was very shy, almost introverted. The first public speech I had to give was in Grade 5, and the experience left me blotchy and gasping for air between sentences. Many sick days resulted from assignments where teachers expected me to do an oral presentation. I was certainly never going to hold down a job where I would be expected to speak in front of a class of students.

Over the years I've been many types of nurse: a cardiac nurse, a public health nurse, a camp nurse, a nurse practitioner. One of my hobbies is collecting *Harlequin*-style nurse books with titles of jobs I've never had, like *Cruise Ship Nurse, Settlement Nurse, Nurse with Wings, District Nurse, Mountaineer Nurse*.

For the last seventeen years I have called myself a street nurse. It's a term coined by a homeless man who one day hollered across the street corner at Sherbourne and Dundas in downtown Toronto: "Hey, street nurse!" It was a huge compliment – not unlike a homeless man calling his close friend on the street his street brother, or sister.

In 1989 there were once maybe four or five of us. Today there are more than a hundred street nurses across the country. George Crust, who has been

Cathy in Grade 2, 1960

homeless, and has faced his own share of physical and mental health challenges, is probably speaking for tens of thousands of recipients of those street nurses' care, when he emphatically states: "I really like the way they do their nursing!"

Street nursing is brave and creative, though it shouldn't have to exist in the first place. It includes dressing a wound under a highway overpass, documenting police-inflicted injuries, treating frostbite, providing intravenous rehydration to patients in shelters during a Norwalk virus outbreak, constantly seeking donations like Gatorade to counter dehydration, and inventing new ways to use duct tape (to mend the soles of shoes, or repair tent-like structures).

I continue to use the term street nurse because it's so descriptive. It doesn't confuse the public like so many of our other nursing job titles like public health nurse, community health nurse, or nurse practitioner. Street nurse – it tells a story of how things today are different than they used to be. It explains in two simple words – street nurse – that this country has a new nursing specialty – homelessness, and this, I suggest to you, is obscene. I'm not a politician, an economist, or an urban planner. I'm a nurse, a street nurse, and what I see "downstream" in society necessitates that I look "upstream" to find the root of the problem. The necessity for street nurses necessitates that our nursing be concerned with politics.

Over the course of my career as a nurse, I've been part of two worlds. In the first world my work was somewhat predictable – monitoring heart rhythms on a cardiology floor, assisting doctors with physicals in a downtown executive medical practice, performing well-baby checkups, offering birth control counselling in a community health centre, and my favourite – home visits to seniors. In the second world, as a street nurse, the conditions I see are not only unjust, they are cause for national shame: an old woman living and dying in a car, a senior sheltering below a bridge, another dying from tuberculosis, a young girl burned to death in her squat. A constant litany of infections and illness: frostbite injuries, malnutrition, dehydration, pneumonias, chronic diarrhea, hepatitis, HIV infection, skin infections from bedbug bites. But perhaps the hardest to treat is the emotional and mental trauma, what I call deprivation of the human spirit. It's evident on the faces and in the body language of homeless people, so reminiscent of the photographs taken during the Depression years in the United States, such as "Migrant Mother" by Dorothea Lange. These faces I've seen – barely surviving, pale, tired, despairing... hungry. How do you nurse *that*? How do you relieve *that* pain?

Why would I begin as a nurse in one world and end up in another? Well, I didn't plan it. It wasn't a spiritual calling, nor was it politically motivated, or driven by social justice leanings, although I had been involved in the peace movement and the women's movement. I was simply drawn to the corner of Sherbourne and Dundas in downtown Toronto because a pioneering nurse named Dilin Baker was making waves in the development of nursing and health care for people who were homeless. She founded Street Health, a grassroots nursing clinic. The idea of working in an organization where I could fully nurse, and not depend on what doctors thought I could or couldn't do, was very appealing.

Dilin had taken an international health course in preparation for work overseas. While volunteering at All Saints Church she was asked by a group of homeless people at Sherbourne and Dundas to help with their problems obtaining health care. By transposing the principles of health care that she would have applied in Africa, to the homeless community in Toronto, she was able to start making a difference. It's called primary health care and it's straightforward, really: be grounded in the community and involve members of the community in decision-making; respond to the community's health care needs in an appropriate fashion; be consistent and reliable; and look upstream.

She ran clinics, with volunteer nurses, in shelters and drop-ins, for several years, until she embarrassed the Ontario Liberal government sufficiently to force them to provide funding. She's the only nurse I know who thought nothing of taking the Minister of Health out for lunch to tell her quite bluntly what was going on, and what the Minister should do about it. I liked the waves she was making – challenging barriers to health care that existed for people who were homeless, confronting widespread discrimination in the health care sector, and insisting that our role as nurses wasn't just to soak the feet and put the bandages on, but also to look for the root causes. I always thought of Mary Magdalene, as we passed the church altar to empty the basin in the bathroom. Other times you could imagine what a nurse might be doing in a refugee camp without enough supplies, with no running water nearby, and a never-ending line of people waiting to see you.

It was there, during the course of nursing clinics in All Saints Church at Sherbourne and Dundas, known as "the four corners" or "the corner," that I cut my teeth as a street nurse. Things shocked me initially, in fact, pretty much all the time: seeing a patient who hadn't eaten all day, another who had slept outside all night, a man who'd had heart surgery ten days earlier and was discharged back to a shelter, an elderly man who had been raped outside a shelter, a woman with her sick child who needed a note for the shelter saying her child was ill and needed extra juice. Eventually these jarring experiences, disturbing as they were, became a constant background – like white noise.

There is a parable about a health care worker visiting a developing country. Standing on a riverbank she sees a few bodies floating by. She quickly sounds an alert and begins pulling the bodies out of the river. She applies first aid and resuscitates one person, but as soon as she looks up there are more bodies coming down the river. She and her companions are soon exhausted from pulling bodies out. Many of them are beyond hope of survival. Then it occurs to the would-be rescuers to look upstream to see what on earth is pushing the bodies in.

I was on a huge learning curve. During these years I developed a lot of knowledge and experience in everything from treating wound infections, to mental health issues, to how to scavenge for clinic supplies. Many of the homeless people I met had so much talent, fight, imagination, and creativity, but they were trapped in their situations. Everywhere there were reminders that I was nursing in a community that was cut off, shunned by the rest of the world. Forty percent of the people did not have an Ontario Health Card despite being eligible. Banks turned them away, so people were forced to use Money Marts to cash their government cheques. And worst of all, police, physicians, and welfare workers often treated the homeless abusively.

I graduated from the Toronto General Hospital School of Nursing, my mother's alma mater. We wore white uniforms, stockings, and caps, and while studying we had to live in residence. The schooling was disciplined. In fact, the program was called "training." We learned that the essence of nursing was caring. We were taught that nursing

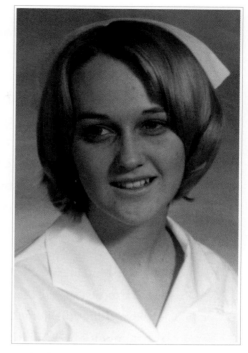

Cathy, first year at Toronto General Hospital School of Nursing, 1971

was a science, but also an art, and there were theories in abundance to back up both views. After a number of years nursing in the community I decided to go to Ryerson Polytechnic Institute (now Ryerson University) to obtain a degree in nursing so that I could work as a Nurse Practitioner. Here I was introduced to concepts of nursing leadership, nursing theory, nursing diagnoses, and political theories. I am very proud that this degree is a Bachelor of Applied Arts in Nursing – it suggests that it's valuable for nurses to have a well-rounded education, including courses in sociology and the arts.

My experience as a street nurse has forced me to rely less on nursing theory and nursing research and more on economics, truth, power, and politics. I prefer to think of nursing as a dance, a subtle and intricate weaving of movements that are about witnessing, attending to meaning, and when necessary, leaping into the fray to grab what should be given. For if politics is about the distribution of limited resources, I learned that nothing is ever freely given. You have to fight for it.

I had the good fortune to be mentored by nurses and non-nurses alike, including former city councillor Roger Hollander, housing activist Michael Shapcott, and outreach worker Beric German, who showed me the delicate and sometimes blunt ways to fight for what was right. I learned that different situations call for different strategies.

I learned that the fight sometimes took the form of action-based research, like the 1992 "Street Health Report," praised by the World Health Organization, or of formal deputations to a city committee, such as the Board of Health. These measures located the severity of homeless people's health, and the barriers to health, on the radar, and eventually led to significant policy changes like making sure homeless people could obtain an Ontario Health Card through community-based kiosks.

Sometimes it involved working within the legal system at coroners' inquests, such as the "Freezing Deaths Inquest" or the "Tuberculosis Inquest." At times it was more important to hold our own public inquiry. "One Is Too Many" (referring to homeless deaths) was an inquiry held in a drop-in centre in All Saints Church, that featured a panel of prominent people, including journalist Michael Valpy and actor Sarah Polley, who heard evidence exposing the severity of homelessness and related deaths in the city.

There were always letters to the editor, articles and opinion pieces, press conferences, and tours where we took members of the media into places they wouldn't normally go – into parks, under bridges, unsafe rooming houses, basement shelters.

And there were moments of pure passion when a heated discussion with a city councillor, a mayor, or a coroner was caught by a TV camera that happened to be very close by.

What all these actions share is the basic formula: witness + honesty + speaking out = the right thing to do. When I look back I realize that just about everything that homeless people have won, whether it be changes in policy, or funding, has resulted from these types of actions. Nothing was granted simply because it was the right thing to do.

Although I had the experience of being free to speak out, I also faced, more times than I care to remember, the experience of being silenced. For a shy girl who had grown into someone compelled to speak out, this caused great moral anguish. I know that many of my colleagues faced similar silencing, especially during the Mike Harris years in Ontario. One day my manager at a community health centre instructed me that I was not allowed to do a media interview about the risk of tuberculosis in the homeless population. Another day, I was told that Citytv's Adam Vaughan, a respected journalist, was not allowed to set foot in the lobby to meet me for a prearranged appointment on a subject related to homelessness. These experiences frustrated me to no end. The day I found myself sneaking into a parked car in a dark alleyway to do a radio interview with the CBC about tuberculosis was the day I realized I was in serious trouble as a nurse if I was going to stay truthful to what I was witnessing.

People often ask me how I sustain myself and avoid burning out. I tell them that we celebrate our wins. Despite a worsening homeless situation, there have been many: several closed or empty hospitals and federal armouries have been repeatedly used for emergency shelter; some of these same buildings have been designated for social housing; new shelter standards have been introduced that more closely meet the United Nations standards for refugee camps; funding has increased for TB screening and follow-up; within forty-eight hours of the 2002 Tent City eviction, housing was established for more than a hundred people who had been living there; one year after the Toronto Disaster Relief Committee's declaration that homelessness was a national disaster, the federal government initiated a homeless strategy that provided hundreds of millions of dollars for emergency assistance to organizations serving the homeless in cities across the country, including Halifax, Montreal, Winnipeg, and Calgary. These are some of the large-scale successes. We also celebrate incremental wins every day.

This is my first book and it has a lot to do with the theme of my daughter Idella's first book. She called hers *The Adventures of My Blanket*. She was eight and her story chronicled, with crayon illustrations, the secret life of her "softy blanket": a shark attack ("I couldn't believe it. My blanket saved my life!"); a frightening visit to the hospital for an operation ("One day my blanket got a rip."); a first day at school ("My friends laughed at it – who ever heard of a blanket learning?"); and the sudden and traumatic melting of best friend snowman ("Suddenly the snowman was gone, and all that was left of him was a big puddle.").

Her book closes with, "The look on my blanket's face said, 'Anything can happen!'" No judgment, just wonder at what goes on in the world.

I felt a lot like that blanket when I realized, very early on as a street nurse, that the right to a home is not granted equally to all Canadians. This may sound naïve, but it's the truth. I was working as a street nurse in 1993 when the federal Conservative government cancelled all new spending for our national housing program. I hate to admit it, but I was oblivious to the decision at that time. The entire housing program was decimated. In some provinces it was a double whammy when they cancelled their provincial housing programs as well. That's what happened in Ontario in 1995, when the Conservative government of Mike Harris cut 17,000 units of housing that were already under development. Units that could have housed up to 40,000 people, including families with children.

Most of us have a softy blanket, some form of gentle protection against the scary and upsetting things that happen in life. It might take the form of family, a friend, or a lover, a talent or hobby we retreat to for comfort or inspiration like music, theatre, or even daydreams. However, we're all more at risk when we lose our societal softy blanket, the social safety net that ensures that when all else fails, systems and programs are in place to protect us. This became evident to me as I witnessed the aftermath of the housing cuts: longer waiting lists for affordable housing, people who were newly homeless and still in shock, the increased need for blankets and sleeping bags, churches opening their basements to provide emergency shelter.

The following year, 1996, was a tragic year, but it shaped a movement. On a cold night in January, a homeless man named Brent Simms died in his sleeping bag on a sidewalk. He had been run over by a car in Toronto's upscale Yorkville.

Within months three more homeless men – Eugene Upper, Irwin Anderson, and Mirsalah-Aldin Kompani – froze to death on Toronto streets. They were our first cluster of homeless deaths, and the news stunned Canadians. How could this have happened in our country? Their deaths enraged a homeless man named Richard Roy, who challenged downtown outreach workers Beric German and Gaetan Heroux to do something. Their response marked a revival of activism around street deaths and homelessness. I joined them, and we began organizing and demonstrating. We created a coalition of twenty-six Toronto agencies and called it the Toronto Coalition against Homelessness (TCAH). The Coalition came together with unprecedented strength and fought for, and was granted, standing at what became known as the Freezing Deaths Inquest. The group retained activist lawyer Peter Rosenthal and obtained legal test case funding.

This concept of using the courts for a political struggle was based on the earlier work of a coalition called Housing Not Hostels, that had participated in the 1986 inquest into the death of Drina Joubert, a woman who froze to death in the back of a truck at Sherbourne and Dundas. My long-time friend and colleague Beric German was there when her body was found. Police asked him to keep silent. He said, "I think not," and proceeded to call the media. The former fashion model's death made front-page news and shocked Torontonians. The Joubert Inquest was the foundation for numerous political wins: the development and funding of an innovative mental health Hostel Outreach Program (HOP) to reach homeless men and women; a 9 percent average increase in welfare rates; and new affordable housing. Project 3000, as it was known, combined three thousand new units of affordable housing with support services. Under this provincial program, single Ontarians became eligible for social housing for the first time. To this day, people live in those units.

During the five-week Freezing Deaths Inquest we filled the courtroom, we served lunch every day outside on the sidewalk, and we fought for the right for homeless people to be expert witnesses. Only Melvin Tipping, whom you will meet in this book, won that right. Despite Coroner Naiberg's persistent refusal to allow the word housing to be used, the five-person jury adopted all of the Coalition's recommendations. To the Coroner's question, "By what means did the men die?" the jury stated: "Homelessness."

Tragically, the recommendations that would have prevented more deaths – funding affordable housing and supports – have not been acted upon to any significant degree by the various levels of government. While the Freezing Deaths Inquest may not have created policy reform, it did help fuel a hot public debate.

In November of the same year, Dorothea Jakob, also a nurse, convinced me to join her at the Temagami old-growth forest protest camp for my first experience of winter camping. I have to admit I was terrified of the cold. I secretly worried whether I would succumb to frostbite or hypothermia.

We doubled our sleeping bags one inside the other and placed foam insulators between them and the ground. Each night we boiled water over an open fire to fill hot water bottles to tuck into our sleeping bags. We stayed warm as long as we didn't have to get up to go to the bathroom. I was reminded that none of these survival tactics were options for homeless people I knew back in the city.

I returned to work smug that I had survived my winter camping experience, but skeptical about our obsession with sleeping bags as an emergency remedy to homelessness. I continued to give out sleeping bags to homeless people, but I began to look at the bags differently and pay attention to their specs. One of the most common bags we gave out was called Expedition, and it had a temperature rating of 0° C. It had polyester filling (not down) and a nylon shell. Occasionally I would see a bag that was safe for –10° C. I only once saw a Gore-Tex bag (safe for –20° C), and that had been donated by a camper. Safe I guess, if you're not run over, or attacked, or have serious health concerns, or it doesn't get extremely cold. In the winter of 2004–2005, Toronto had twenty-six "cold weather alert" days, indicating that the temperature was –15° C or below, not counting wind chill.

Year after year the need for sleeping bags kept increasing, and there was always a shortage. Then, in 2000, John Andras, a businessman and self-described Bay Street "suit" who had been instrumental in founding the Toronto Disaster

Relief Committee and Project Warmth, made a carefully considered but surprising decision. At its peak, Project Warmth had collected and distributed thirty-five thousand blankets and sleeping bags in Toronto alone. The average street life of a bag is about three days: they get wet, soiled, or thrown into the garbage by city clean-up crews. John let me know that Project Warmth had decided to discontinue its massive sleeping bag collection and distribution program. He felt it was no longer an adequate response.

The same week, Christ Church Deer Park, which operated an Out of the Cold program run by volunteers, announced the end of their Saturday night shelter. They were going to focus on developing affordable housing. I was a hundred percent behind both of these decisions, and remember crying with relief. Why? Because these relief efforts had been normalizing two very abnormal practices. Homeless people continued to sleep outdoors through the Canadian winter, year after year. The very public sight of homeless people huddled inside bright red, green, and blue sleeping bags on grates and sidewalks in this city eventually numbed the public consciousness. The other, more hidden practice was the forced nightly migration of hundreds of people from church basement to church basement in search of a place to sleep.

Sleeping bag distribution and church basements had become an excuse for City Hall not to enact emergency by-laws to open more shelters. The province and the coroner's office were nowhere to be seen, even after the first attacks on homeless people lying vulnerable in their sleeping bags.

The issue of charitable relief efforts in times of crisis has been controversial. Charity is certainly necessary in the immediate crisis until the appropriate level of government can respond. But for fifteen years? What we have witnessed in Canada is the government's prolonged reliance on volunteer groups to provide increasingly complicated types of aid, with no sign of proper funding for the social service sector, let alone housing relief.

In Toronto, Project Warmth, and Christ Church Deer Park threw the responsibility to shelter and house people back to government. They were later joined by St. Andrew's Presbyterian Church, which decided to close its overnight Out of the Cold program.

Cardboard box homeless shelter in Toronto's financial district, 1999

Street beds aren't real beds, mats on a floor aren't a bedroom, and sleeping bags sure aren't a softy blanket. Sleeping bags should not be our country's national housing program.

Today in most communities across Canada the shelters are at capacity. When I visit Sudbury, Winnipeg, Edmonton, Sarnia, or York Region, I hear the same thing. There are never enough spaces for homeless families with children. They are routinely put into welfare motels. There are long waiting lists for affordable housing every place I visit. I remember the sinking feeling I had when conditions reached a point where all I could do as a street nurse was to give an elderly man a bus ticket to get to his favourite spot for the night, be it a hot air grate, or a bank machine vestibule. I testified to that fact at the Freezing Deaths Inquest. I began to see cardboard boxes used, not for make-believe playhouses, but for human shelter, and also flattened to shield a sleeping body from the damp, cold pavement.

My all-time favourite protest sign is a flattened cardboard box. In bold black letters it carries this message: "It's a shame when GE does a better job housing the homeless than the government of Canada." Ironically, cardboard did turn into a temporary solution when we began to install pressed corrugated cardboard "disaster housing" on the city waterfront for people at Tent City. Toronto public health monies helped pay for portable toilets, but it wasn't until after the brutal evictions at Tent City that Toronto came up with housing for more than a hundred Tent City residents.

One of my first impressions as a street nurse in downtown Toronto was that there were an awful lot of people with rich Maritime accents at the corner of Sherbourne and Dundas. And boy, were they homesick! Like the canary in the mineshaft, these Maritimers were signalling a warning. When economic conditions in smaller communities are bad, there is always a forced migration to larger communities. So when plants close, when social and community supports are cut, when it becomes harder to qualify for employment insurance, when welfare rates are slashed, when the minimum wage stays the same and the cost of living keeps going up, and most of all when housing and feeding yourself or your family becomes impossible – all roads lead out of town, but not necessarily to a better place. They usually lead to a big city: Halifax, Montreal, Ottawa, Toronto, Winnipeg, Regina, Saskatoon, Edmonton, Calgary, Vancouver.

Back in the early 1970s a Canadian movie called *Goin' Down the Road* told the story of a couple of Maritimers migrating to Toronto looking for adventure, and more importantly, work. Sadly, it is still relevant. In downtown Toronto I continue to meet francophones from rural Quebec, First Nations peoples from the north and west, people from rural areas whose farms have gone bankrupt, and people who come from smaller communities that lack social services like shelters, or who are too embarrassed about using them in their small town.

The only difference today is that the road leading out is paved by free trade, cuts in social assistance and employment insurance, privatization, and discrimination.

Homelessness took a terrible turn for the worse in the mid- to late 1990s. In fact, in some emergency shelters, it became apparent that even the most basic standards, such as the United Nations standards for refugee camps, were not being met. I remember taking then city councillor Jack Layton on an impromptu midnight visit to such a shelter. We saw 120 men and women on the floor, sleeping on mats in an airless basement. Visibly upset, he turned to me as we left the building and told me, "You usually only see that many bodies in a picture in a book – bodies laid out for identification after some horrible act of violence."

During the '90s I also saw many new faces, men and women who would seek me out as the nurse in the drop-in centre to ask a question to which the more seasoned homeless person already knew the answer, like "Which church basement is open tonight?" They would often apologize and say, "You know, I don't usually come to a place like this." The shell-shocked expressions on their faces told me that they had never imagined they would end up in a drop-in centre, or needing the services of a shelter.

Street nurses and outreach workers began to see clusters of tuberculosis infection, clusters of homeless deaths, and a doubling of the number of homeless people in drop-in centres, within months of the 1995 provincial welfare cuts. We began to see people who were still homeless after ten years, and at the same time lots of new faces, often as a result of evictions. Where once I could find housing for someone with a serious health problem like a brain tumour or a stroke, I no longer could. Vitamins were more and more necessary, and nurses were forced to solicit donations from pharmaceutical companies. Signs of malnutrition and starvation were apparent everywhere. My nursing interventions more and more often included giving someone a bus ticket to get to a grate at the end of the day. Where I used to see eight to ten people in a two-hour outreach clinic, I now saw twenty. This is what I call the beginning of "piecemeal health care." I added duct tape, Ensure, socks, mittens, and granola bars to the Mountain Equipment Co-op knapsack that I used for nursing outreach. Meanwhile, my file on deaths got thicker. I began with little notes to myself about a patient who had died, clipped newspaper articles on homeless deaths, added pictures I'd taken of people – and slowly it grew to be my largest file.

I knew enough to understand that this scene was happening not just in Toronto. Toronto was simply one of many urban centres across Canada, reminding us of the dangerous economic and health conditions throughout the country.

I often feel guilty saying how much I love the winter, because the cold weather always signals more hardships for the homeless people I work with. But it's because of the weather that I had a nursing epiphany.

It was the gruelling 1998 ice storm in Eastern Ontario and Quebec that shocked me into realizing that homelessness was a disaster on an even greater scale. Glued to television coverage of the storm, I watched the government's response with intense interest, and what I witnessed challenged my conscience deeply: families forced to live in crowded school gymnasiums for weeks on end; the elderly stranded without their medications; no place for personal belongings or private, personal space. Everyone getting tired, cranky, sick. I seriously contemplated going to Kingston or Montreal to help in the relief efforts. Despite never having worked as a nurse in an official disaster zone, I was convinced I could contribute. At that time I had eleven years' experience working in crowded drop-ins and shelters, providing health care to homeless people in emergency conditions – often working alone or without running water, proper supplies, or light. I was adaptable and effective in a crisis. I worried, though. Was my French good enough to get by in Quebec? Would I be able to get time off work to go? These questions plagued me daily. Yet the more I followed the ice storm coverage, the more I was convinced I had to go.

As soon as I made the decision I was hit with a wave of emotion – my gut told me something was seriously wrong. I realized that to go was to deny that homeless people here were living in a disaster! I realized that the images on television that had moved me were the daily, hellish circumstances of homeless people's lives. Homeless people spending three hours in one drop-in until it closes, then moving on to the next one that's open. The constant line-ups for meagre resources – lining up to use the phone, to see a nurse or lawyer, to get a bus ticket, for food, for a shower, or the bathroom. Then wondering where you'll sleep that night, which church basement is open, again getting in line, wondering who you'll be sleeping next to, will there be enough blankets, food? I remembered that I had recently been looking at disaster and relief literature in hopes of getting some tips on how to deal with the problems I was seeing in my work. I was overcome with grief and nausea as the truth hit home.

This was my nursing epiphany: Homelessness is a *man-made* disaster.

> from
>
> ## "A Worker's Speech to a Doctor"
>
> by Bertolt Brecht
>
> When we come to you
> Our rags are torn off us
> And you listen all over our naked body.
> As to the cause of our illness
> One glance at our rags would
> Tell you more. It is the same cause that
>   wears out
> Our bodies and our clothes.
>
> The pain in our shoulder comes
> You say, from the damp; and this is also
>   the reason
> For the stain on the wall of our flat.
> So tell us:
> Where does the damp come from?

When we face a natural disaster like an ice storm or a flood, the community and the state kick in. Generally, we witness a rapid humanitarian and government response. There is no argument about who has become homeless, or who is deserving or not deserving. We help people return to their homes, and we compensate victims for their loss and suffering. Politicians and prominent community leaders visit the disaster zone to see for themselves and to offer consolation and promises of relief.

The comparison of the situation of people made homeless by policy rather than, for example, by the weather, was a painful reminder to me that homeless people, no matter where they are in Canada, fundamentally have no home to go back to and no central "heart" that is a support or a base. Disasters could no longer be stereotyped or dismissed simply as the end damage from floods, ice storms, or earthquakes. The disaster that the housing crisis created had left many without a home for years. That disaster was visible if I looked: people were on our street corners, on sidewalks and grates, in ravines, and hidden in motels and hotels, and shelters, across the country.

Unlike other disaster victims, homeless people's emergency shelter stays were not temporary. Many families, children, and the elderly had been stuck in these shelters for five to ten years. For couples without children who wanted to stay together, sleeping outside was often the only option. A growing number of people were forced to use Out of the Cold or Inn from the Cold. These are programs run by volunteers, and usually connected with a faith group. They operate on a night-by-night basis in the winter months, and people who are homeless are invited in as "guests." With few exceptions, there were no politicians or community leaders touring the homeless disaster, offering consolation or solutions. The one exception I know about was Bruce McLeod, the former moderator of the United Church of Canada, who stayed one night at Seaton House and later wrote and spoke out about the experience.

For people who were homeless in Canada, the electricity was not going to magically turn on, giving them the "freedom" to go home, back to work, or school. There would be no compensation for suffering and loss. They were essentially just stuck. All major cities were facing escalating numbers of homeless people, many of whom had been forced to migrate. The evidence pointed to a formidable national problem.

Disasters, I learned, are not restricted to developing or war-torn countries, nor are they limited to natural causes such as fire, ice, or flooding. Additional research by a friend and retired professor, Norm Feltes, verified that homelessness qualified as a social welfare disaster. In retrospect, I realized that all the signs of a disaster had been evident: more than a quarter of a million people affected, clusters of infections, the rise in overall morbidity including malnutrition, a resurgence of old diseases like tuberculosis, and a rapid rise in the number of homeless deaths. Like internally displaced persons during a natural disaster or civil war, people moved into remote areas, such as ravines, and established tent cities and squatter camps – other forms of community for survival. At the same time, I was witnessing evidence of widespread suffering and exhaustion among homeless people, including anxiety, sleep loss, depression, and a pervasive lack of hope. Among the front-line workers, the group one might compare to rescue workers in a disaster, I saw depleted energy, higher rates of illness, and burnout.

Given the scope of the problem, we should have seen federal relief and reconstruction efforts. Instead, homeless people were abandoned by their governments.

I still get asked, "Who makes up the homeless? Are they all mentally ill, or are they homeless because of drug use?" People are surprised to learn that the only thing in common among homeless people today in Canada is that they have been "dehoused," a concept made very clear by Professor David Hulchanski in an article he wrote called "Did the Weather Cause Canada's Mass Homelessness?" He outlines how people have been dehoused through processes like welfare and employment insurance cuts, policies that make evictions easier, and, of course, the cancellation of federal and provincial housing programs that would have added tens of thousands of new housing units per year across the country. The end result? A social safety net so riddled with holes that people are slipping through at an alarming rate.

In a local restaurant in the St. Lawrence Market neighbourhood in Toronto, near where I live, Beric German and I often got together to discuss the horrific situations we were seeing in our work. For Beric, there were constant reminders of what he had seen as a young man when he did relief work in Bangladesh. We were both affected by the daily traumas we witnessed – I call it vicarious trauma. We coped by talking. In fact, I think maybe one of the reasons we have been able to continue is that we have been able to talk about the underlying political pathology, or ideology, bounce ideas around, strategize, and ultimately develop new campaigns. Every conversation I've had with Beric has been a political awakening. I have a poster at home commemorating the 1989 Montreal massacre of fourteen women that says "First mourn, then work for change." Beric and I mourned but also got really angry. And then we went back to the work.

In the spring of 1998, just months after the big ice storm, our conversations took on a heightened sense of desperation regarding the local scene. I liken Beric's work to that of a film director: he sees the big picture and can imagine and create the frames that follow. I'm part of the production.

Years earlier, in 1987, there had been attempts to declare Toronto a homeless disaster zone because homelessness was a public health emergency. Former Metro councillor Roger Hollander (to whom I was married at the time) brought this motion forward to Metro Council. Ultimately, it failed. It's no surprise that Roger attempted this. For years he had listened to me describing what I'd seen in the course of my day.

Beric and I felt we had to try again. Together, we decided to frame homelessness as a man-made disaster – in fact, to issue a declaration that homelessness in Canada was a national disaster. Over the next few months we created a campaign that was both precise and passionate. Casting is everything. We brought together a cast of colleagues from various walks of life who believed what we believed – that homelessness in Canada was a violation of human rights. They included lawyer Peter Rosenthal, housing activist Michael Shapcott, housing researcher David Hulchanski, progressive real estate developer David Walsh, Bay Street financial expert and Rotarian John Andras, activist/priest/former MP Don (then Dan) Heap, Anglican priest Jeannie Loughrey, activists Frank Showler and Gaetan Heroux, artist/activist Sherrie Golden, writer Steve Lane, mental health outreach workers Paula Dolezal and Maurice Adongo, and AIDS activists Trevor Gray and Brent Patterson. We called ourselves the Toronto Disaster Relief Committee, and we wrote the State of Emergency Declaration. We issued this on October 8, 1998, to a packed audience of several hundred people in the Church of the Holy Trinity in downtown Toronto. That morning the *Toronto Star* headline read "Plight of the Homeless: A National Disaster."

The State of Emergency Declaration says:

> The homeless situation is worsening daily at an alarming rate, as the factors creating it remain unchecked. Any delay in firmly and massively responding will only contribute to compounding the present crisis of suffering and death which is already an epidemic which no civilized society can tolerate.

At the crux of the Declaration was the profound belief that homelessness constituted a national disaster:

> We call on all levels of government to declare homelessness a national disaster requiring emergency humanitarian relief. We urge that they immediately develop and implement a National Homelessness Relief and Prevention Strategy using disaster relief funds both to provide the homeless with immediate health protection and housing and to prevent further homelessness.

At the press conference, Professor Ursula Franklin solemnly declared, "Homelessness is a national disaster. We have the legal and technical means to end it." The Declaration called for immediate short-term relief measures as well as the 1 percent solution – the demand that all levels of government spend an additional 1 percent of their budgets to build affordable housing. This formula originated from research by University of Toronto professor David Hulchanski. He had researched ten years of funding for housing and discovered that prior to the massive cuts, governments had spent an average of 1 percent of their budget on housing. As housing researcher Michael Shapcott has since added:

Cathy speaking to Ontario Federation of Labour outside Toronto City Hall, 2001

"The 1 percent solution is the first and foremost means to end the homelessness crisis."

The Declaration meant that homelessness and the housing crisis were catapulted onto the national scene. For eleven days straight the front page of the *Toronto Star* covered the crisis. Not long after, they assigned a journalist, Catherine Dunphy, to cover the homeless file full-time. The *Star* was the first media outlet in Canada to assign a journalist full-time to homeless issues.

On October 28, 1998, Metropolitan Toronto Council, in a 53–1 vote, endorsed what came to be known as the Disaster Declaration. The Municipalities of Ottawa-Carleton, Vancouver, Victoria, Peel, Durham Region, and the Big City Mayors Caucus of the Federation of Canadian Municipalities, all followed suit. The Disaster Declaration also captured the imagination of hundreds of organizations, including the Registered Nurses Association of Ontario, St. Michael's Hospital, the International Institute of Concern for Public Health, and the Canadian Auto Workers. Hundreds of community organizations and individuals also signed on.

The following month, in Geneva, the State of Emergency Declaration was delivered to the UN Committee on Economic, Social and Cultural Rights, by Josephine Grey, of the Toronto-based NGO Low Income Families Together, and Bruce Porter, of the Centre for Equality Rights in Accommodation.

The rest is history.

I believe that much of this work has had a profound effect on international, legal, and moral understanding of homelessness in Canada. Homelessness is now established as a national issue and the language used to describe it includes the word disaster. Disasters are no longer understood to be limited to developing countries, or to chemical spills, or to extreme weather.

Homelessness is fundamentally a human rights issue. Despite this evident truth, the federal government continued to pay it only lip service. In 1999, Prime Minister Chrétien appointed a Minister Responsible for Homelessness, Claudette Bradshaw. This was the first time that a federal cabinet minister had been given this portfolio – ironic, given that the federal housing minister, Alfonso Gagliano, was given no mandate or budget for an affordable housing program.

Bradshaw was given responsibility for developing a homelessness strategy. Partners in the newly formed National Housing and Homelessness Network (NHHN) agreed to meet the minister throughout Canada and deliver a powerful message: homelessness had become a national disaster, and a new national housing strategy was the solution.

After touring the country, Bradshaw agreed to half the demands from the NHHN. She announced a program called Supporting Communities Partnership Initiative, or SCPI (known as "Skippy"). It included about $750 million over three years, and was geared to short-term services for the homeless. The program was originally limited to ten cities. After pressure from housing and homeless advocacy groups, the federal government expanded the allowable projects from hostels to include some transitional housing. Further pressure from advocates eased the definition of transition, so that SCPI funds could be used to support new housing projects in some parts of the country. This was the first federally funded housing in almost a decade. The federal government also expanded the geographic reach of the program by targeting 80 percent of the funds to ten cities (though only one in all of Atlantic Canada: Halifax), and the remaining 20 percent was divided up throughout the rest of the country.

No new money was added. The existing pie was simply cut into thinner slices. Minister Bradshaw, answering questions from the media at the launch of the homelessness strategy in December of 1999, called it a "first step." The homelessness strategy was designed to make homeless people more comfortable, but it wouldn't make them any less homeless. The few new units of transitional housing squeezed out of this program did hardly anything to stem the growing tide of homelessness. In the February 2000 federal budget, Ottawa announced a $7.5 billion infrastructure program to be cost-shared with the provinces, territories, and municipalities.

The federal government said that part of the funding might go towards housing – subject to agreement by the provinces, territories and municipalities. But in the following months it became clear that almost all of the infrastructure spending would go to spending on water supply and sewers. Housing ended up at the bottom of a long list of other capital projects.

The federal homelessness strategy and the municipal infrastructure program were important initiatives, but neither delivered affordable housing in the amount required by low-income households. Canada needs a fully funded national housing program, with the co-operation of the provinces and territories.

SCPI was renewed in 2003 for a second three-year term. It was renewed in 2006 for one year only. Only days before Christmas 2006, the federal homelessness minister announced $270 million over two years to extend the program. The monies will now be spread even thinner, to more than sixty communities.

The inaction of governments in Canada has long been brought to the attention of the United Nations. In 1999, the Toronto Disaster Relief Committee submitted a report titled "Death on the Streets of Canada" to the United Nations Human Rights Committee in New York. The report stated:

As a direct result of governmental actions and inactions, tens of thousands of people have been forced into substandard housing, into overcrowded and inadequate temporary shelters for the homeless and onto the streets. Increased morbidity and early death have followed.

The government of Canada's actions and lack of action leading to, and failing to prevent, morbidity and death, violate the moral and ethical codes of the nation's religions, the Canadian Charter of Rights and Freedoms, and the federal and provincial human rights codes. We now call on international human rights law for assistance.

The UN Committee's clear response:

The committee is concerned that homelessness has led to serious problems and even death. The committee recommends that the State party take positive measures... to address this serious problem.

Maclean's magazine reported in 2000 that 85 percent of Canadians agreed with the statement that they want to see "increased spending to eliminate homelessness," and a Pollara poll showed homelessness to be one of the top five issues of concern to Canadians.

We witnessed unprecedented public support for Toronto's struggling Tent City. The public generally viewed it as a community simply trying to survive, and a group of people with a pioneering spirit that should be supported. The Tent City squatters were able to articulate why shelters were dangerous to their health. In the face of government inaction, they became respected for creating their own solutions. Tent City became the largest and longest form of civil disobedience by homeless people in Canada since the Great Depression. They won a huge political victory, led by Dri, Nancy Baker, Marty Lang, Brian Boyd, and the Colonel.

Beyond a doubt, the hardest part of my work has been the deaths. I work as a community health nurse, not a palliative care nurse. I'm not working in a literal war zone. But these deaths are no accident. I should not be seeing

Cathy outside Coroners Courts, nervously awaiting TB inquest verdict, 2004

this amount of death. Dr. Stephen Hwang and Dr. Angela Cheung, leading researchers in homelessness, agree. They did studies looking at deaths among homeless men and women in Toronto, and found that on average they died at a much higher rate than would be expected in the general population.

No one should be dying homeless in this country, even of natural causes. In this book you'll meet Melvin Tipping, who has made this point on the witness stand and on a regular basis. I thought Toronto was the hotspot for homeless deaths, but everywhere I've travelled in the last two years I've heard the same thing. Whether it's Ottawa, Sudbury, Winnipeg, Edmonton, Vancouver – homeless people and front-line workers are devastated by the loss of life. Dead: a pregnant aboriginal woman within sight of the House of Commons in Ottawa; an elderly woman in a car; a young girl in a fire in a squat; a man with AIDS; a man beaten to death in his sleeping bag; a man found drowned in Lake Ontario not far from his tent-like structure, where his construction helmet and boots still hung; a man on a grate within sight of the Premier of Ontario's office; a man in an underground parking lot... I could go on and on. Sometimes the Coroner's Office reports a homeless death as being "from natural causes." Well, it's not normal or natural to die homeless, even if it is from cancer or old age.

Canada now has a total of two shelters with palliative care components. Homeless deaths are preventable. People in this country are dying for a home.

A few years ago, a woman who lived in a car with her elderly mother asked to meet with me. She told me, "The public just doesn't get it. They walk by the person on the grate, or panhandling, and they don't realize that person was once a worker, maybe not so long ago. That person had an occupation." She reminded me of the nurse who died on the street, of the skilled tradespeople who were homeless. She told me I had to keep telling people this so they would take action.

She was right. Over the years I've watched the labelling get worse. They are called "the homeless," or worse, the "chronically homeless," or the "chronics," "guests," "street people," "addicts," "winos," even "squirrel eaters." We are told that they "choose" to sleep outside. An artist chooses to be an artist, a doctor chooses to be a doctor. No one chooses to be homeless. In this book you'll meet Bonnie and Kerre Briggs, who lay all the myths and assumptions to rest.

Homeless people are frequently portrayed on the grate, on the ground, prostrate, depersonalized. In this book you'll meet James Kagoshima, who taught me the necessity of engaging homeless people in outreach and advocacy, and showed me the potential for involving them in a substantial way to effect change.

Most cultures have had homelessness. It's an old concept. But for the most part, society was able to find a way to counter that age-old problem – with food, with social programs like income assistance and housing. Sadly, we seem to be going backwards. People who are poor are increasingly marginalized and stigmatized. This translates into prejudice, hate crimes, and hate legislation. Our language about homelessness reflects this. We label people who are homeless, and that allows us to depersonalize them. Instead, we should try to understand the real nature of the problem. People who are homeless are not "street people," and the solution we proffer should not symbolically be that of a broom, sweeping people off the street with criminalizing laws. In this book a number of people touch on policing, but Kevin Clarke's voice is the most determined regarding his experience.

Let's call people without housing what they really are – dehoused people, or economic refugees, or displaced persons. That's what the United Nations would call them.

I have met and known thousands of people who were homeless, and I can't think of one who deserved it, who chose it, or who couldn't have done just

Members of National Housing and Homelessness Network celebrating signing of the Affordable Housing Agreement, 2001

fine if the right type of housing and supports had been there. No one is hard to house; it's the right housing that's hard to find. And it could be so easy.

Some of the homeless people I've had the privilege of knowing, I've also had the privilege of working with. They have not received the recognition they deserve for the extraordinary acts of advocacy they have engaged in while living in less than optimum circumstances. I want to introduce you to some of them in this book.

They are homeless activists, and they have fought for housing – for themselves and for others. They have raised their voices to call for a national housing program – with poetry, with speeches at press conferences and rallies, with evidence at inquests, with media interviews. By building structures and squats, they have demonstrated that they are determined to build a home.

They are brave and spirited. They have talents and imagination. They are stubborn and determined. They are upright. They are fighting for a home.

They are dying for a home.

CHAPTER 2

MELVIN TIPPING

EXPERT WITNESS

Melvin outside Coroners Courts where he had been a witness, 2006

Although I was Melvin's nurse for about fifteen years, I can't lay claim to being his favourite.

That honour goes to a nurse named Wenda. My friend and colleague Morris Wolfe, with whom I first interviewed Melvin, skilfully drew that little tidbit out when he asked Melvin, "So if Cathy and Wenda were both in the clinic, which one would you head for?" Melvin's too quick answer, "Wenda," was followed by a chuckle. I'm just glad it wasn't the scenario, "If you were stuck in a canoe with people drowning in the water, and you could only save one person, which one would it be?" Seriously, Melvin credits Wenda with helping him re-establish his life, and she sure did.

I first met Melvin in the early '90s when Wenda and I worked at Street Health in downtown Toronto. Street Health was probably the first nursing clinic in Canada that was reaching out to provide health care to homeless people. It was located in All Saints Church at Sherbourne and Dundas, in what I call the epicentre of homelessness in Canada, and it's where I "cut my teeth" as a street nurse.

It's interesting for me to reflect back on my first memories and impressions of Melvin, because in some ways Melvin typified who and what I thought a homeless person would be all about. He was in his fifties, single, and unemployed. He was a self-described alcoholic. He definitely had a "colourful history," and was estranged from his family.

At the time I was still a fairly naïve nurse and had no sense of context, or understanding of what income, employment, housing, or simply having friends and family had to do with health.

So, for example, when "Bob" would come in to the clinic wearing a shirt that said "Joe" with a gas station logo on it, I couldn't figure out why he wore a shirt with someone else's name on it, and if he was working in the gas station, why did he need to see a street nurse? Eventually I realized that nearly everyone I saw was obtaining their clothes, second-hand, from Mrs. Sinclair's clothing store in the church basement. They didn't teach me these clues in nursing school.

Little did I know that Melvin would come to personify so much more than my homeless stereotype. Over the years I watched with admiration as he overcame some hard knocks in life. He just kept moving forward. Eventually he got involved in housing advocacy himself, eagerly joining groups I invited him to, such as the Toronto Coalition Against Homelessness. This is the group that called for a coroner's inquest into what became known as the "Three Freezing Deaths" of homeless men, in 1996. Melvin's first-hand knowledge and experiences on the street, his eloquence and his passion for politics and current affairs, made him a natural spokesperson and advocate, and ultimately the only witness with experience in homelessness allowed by the presiding coroner at that inquest.

It was in our job description at Street Health to look beyond the swollen legs and sore feet we soaked. We were expected to examine the larger picture: not just who was in front of us, but how and why. In fact we were ordered to do that "upstream work" by our "Head Nurse," Dilin Baker, and we were expected to research it, speak out about it, and find solutions. This was my dream job.

The so called "bigger picture" was right there unravelling in front of us every day. You couldn't *not* see it. I remember one day at our clinic at the Dixon Hall Shelter we began to see guys from the Inglis Plant. The plant had been closed, the men had lost their jobs, and there they were, their savings used up, and forced to use a shelter. There it was, right in front of me, not the fact that they needed medication for a cold, or had a rash from scabies. My nursing diagnosis: side effect of Free Trade.

It was during these years that I'd begun to pay more attention to politics and what was happening in the economy. I realized I better read several newspapers a day, and that I'd also better read the business section to monitor plant closures and layoffs. Melvin and I had that in common. He read at least five newspapers a day.

Well, Melvin got stuck with me as his nurse when Wenda moved to the Canadian north to work in an outpost, so we got to spend more time together.

He also began frequenting Evangel Hall and the Meeting Place – two west-end drop-ins where I did weekly clinics for ten years. My time with Melvin varied from chastising him about his three-pack-a-day habit, to many wonderful conversations about politics and current affairs. We often had lively exchanges, which were refreshing breaks during my two-hour clinics where I would treat anywhere from fifteen to twenty patients. Melvin closely followed the demise of social programs during the neo-conservative Mike Harris years in Ontario. He also enjoyed commenting on the antics of colourful local politicians such as then Mayor Mel Lastman, and progressive City Councillor Jack Layton. Looking back, I remember Melvin being very discouraged, predicting that senior levels of government would never do anything about housing, and I now realize how prescient he was.

I think he came to see me as an okay nurse, even if I wasn't Wenda.

My biggest nursing coup with Melvin was to convince him to go to St. Mike's emergency room with me, on a day when he was obviously having a stroke in the Evangel Hall drop-in, right in front of me. You didn't have to be much of a nurse to figure that out. He wasn't talking, which was extremely unusual (I quickly learned it was because he couldn't), and he had a "droopy" face and total left-sided body weakness. Amazingly, he didn't complain once about any of these symptoms and refused to see his doctor. You see, it was the Men's Group day – lunch and a movie at Evangel Hall. Melvin did eventually go with me to the Emergency Department, but only after he finished having lunch and watching the movie. The Evangel Hall staff had to twist his arm, telling him, "Cathy will be really mad if you don't go with her." He went, he was admitted, and recovered.

Melvin's stubbornness was evident in so many other ways. Strong-willed and determined, Melvin showed up and sat through every single day of the six-week "Freezing Deaths Inquest" in 1996.

Melvin is now sixty-nine, and involved with programs at Evangel Hall, including the Men's Group, and with COPA (Community Older Persons Alcohol Project). He's been in the same housing Wenda helped him find more than twelve years ago.

Although the years have been hard, his eyes have retained their twinkle, and he remains a political news junkie, always bringing me up-to-date on current political affairs.

At the Tequila Sunrise, a coffee shop on Toronto's Queen Street West across from the Evangel Hall, we met to talk about his life. As if orchestrated to fit our conversation, vibrant piano, opera, and choral music wafted in as the perfect backdrop. Our conversation ended on Brahms' *Requiem*.

– Cathy

I WAS BORN IN WINNIPEG IN 1937. MY MOTHER WAS BORN IN Manchester, England, and my father in Liverpool. They came to Winnipeg when they were very young. We weren't rich and we weren't poor. My father was a banker, a teller. Then he went off to war in 1941 and served in Britain. It was bad then in Canada because they drafted almost everybody. He came home safely. My mother worked as a housekeeper during the war.

I have an older brother and three sisters who are younger. They live in Calgary.

My first memory is when I was about six years old. I got in my first fight and won. In 1954, I had a year of university, I was just seventeen, I was quite smart. I wanted to study social work because I felt sorry for low-income people, the homeless, and the unemployed. But I got in trouble with the law. I stole a coat for my girlfriend because she didn't have one. I was caught, she left me, and I had to do some time.

I was one of the first homeless people in Winnipeg although I didn't think of myself as homeless at the time. I got in an argument with my father and he threw me out. I joined a gang. Most of us slept on the street, wherever we could find a place. In winter, I stayed in stairwells in apartment buildings. That turned out to be practice for me when I later became homeless in Toronto.

In '64 I went to Ontario to work in smaller towns – Oshawa, and then Belleville, because I knew some people there. I stayed five years helping a farmer with his crops and cattle and stuff. It was easy. I've got a strong back.

I left Belleville in '69. I wanted to see Toronto. I'd heard so much about it. Rent was cheap then. Five dollars a week for a room. I'd saved fifty dollars and I rented a room in the east end. There were agencies to help you find work. Or you could line up at Sherbourne and Queen. People in cars and trucks would come by and point and say, "You, you and you." Sometimes you got work, usually hard, physical labour for a day or two and sometimes longer. When it was busy you might get work every day. I worked in construction and I moved furniture. I wasn't feeling sorry for myself. That's the way it goes sometimes. I even worked at the Branson Hospital in North York. Cleaning. Then I got a disease where you turn yellow. Jaundice. I probably got it at work. But I never saw a doctor or collected any benefits.

Being sick put me back on the street again. Someone I knew in the east end let me stay with him for a while. Then I went back to doing hard labour. I was thirty-three or thirty-four then. I could never bring myself to panhandle. I don't think a man should have to do that. Every man should have a chance to work. It's 1971 or '72. I'd work and then spend time with my buddies, having a few beers at the Duke of York at Leslie and Queen. And other east end pubs. I was drinking heavily. But I kept working. I had to work so I could drink.

I got married in '74 in London, Ontario. I was there looking for a job. We stayed in London for a couple of years and had two kids. Then we moved to Peterborough – I knew someone there and we had another kid. Then we broke up and I came back to Toronto. I was homeless again. I'm not in touch with my kids – that's in the past and I've moved forward. I'm at peace about that.

I was in the shelter system a couple of times but I didn't like it. I preferred the street and slept wherever I could. I didn't want to be sleeping with a large group of people. The guys are too close together. You lose stuff. You get robbed. I got bugs in the shelter.

That's how I lived during the '80s and early '90s. I still had hope that I'd get straightened out and sober.

The word "homeless" didn't mean anything to me until much later when I was on the street in Toronto. I had only the little work I did for support.

The Homeless Memorial

When a homeless person died we used to hold a press conference or march to the site of the person's death or to the Mayor's office. Then, so many people were dying, we couldn't respond any longer. For so many reasons. Marching to the locked glass office door of then Mayor Mel Lastman felt useless. Homeless people and activists were increasingly overwhelmed by the grief of it all. We were surrounded by death. We couldn't even convince the City to help create a permanent homeless memorial – like ones we have in the City to honour war vets, or injured workers, or the Chinese immigrants who built Canada's railway, or police killed in the line of duty.

Sara Boyles, at the Church of the Holy Trinity, saw the community grief and worked with members of the congregation to develop a Homeless Memorial. It includes a monthly ceremony held in conjunction with the Toronto Disaster Relief Committee, on the church steps, in the shadow of the Eaton Centre, followed by a meal inside the church. Each month the service varies but candles are always lit,

Sometimes I went to the shelters for meals but it wasn't something I was comfortable with. A lot of the time the food was greasy and too spicy.

I moved off the streets to Cabbagetown where I rented a room for $390 a month. I hated it because it was too hot in the summer and too cold in the winter. There were mice and cockroaches and the landlord took most of my money. He was a good guy then because he would lend you five dollars when you asked but you paid him back ten dollars. In fourteen years of being on the streets I was alone. I had no help until I met a street nurse named Wenda Hickmott. She helped me to get an apartment. Half of the stuff in my apartment Wenda got me: a bed, chair, dresser, dishes, a can opener, and clothing. Finally I had a home. She also linked me to COPA (Community Older Persons Alcohol Program). For the first time since 1973 I was sober and getting help for my drinking problem.

When I first moved into where I live now, my nurse Wenda wanted me to poetry is read, a song is sung, and political statements are made. Names of home-less men and women who have died since the last month are added to the board. The list has grown.

Melvin came to the twenty-four hour vigil at the Church of the Holy Trinity. The event marked the addition of the four hundredth name of a homeless person.

"I knew about thirty or thirty-five of those names," Melvin said, "and I prob-ably know some of the John Does too. Eugene Upper was a nice fellow. I came today to find out how many names were on the memorial list. Four hundred – I was shocked. It's quite a disaster. The City, the Province and agencies are not doing enough. Especially at nighttime, people need more help. I feel quite resolved to keep on helping the homeless to get out of the situation.

We have to continue to fight to get housing. If we let this go another four years, we'll have a lot of problems."

– Cathy

quit drinking, so I quit. She thought I was too old to keep working, and that I needed a rest. That was '94. I was fifty-seven. She's the one who got me the apartment in Metro Housing. This is my twelfth year there.

Once I got housing, I started becoming involved in housing politics and coalitions. The first was called "Housing Not Hostels." I became active in other ways. I talked to the media. I've made presentations at City Hall. I've done informal counselling with people who are new to the street. Some have kids and want answers to where they can find housing.

In the early '90s, there were suddenly more and more homeless people out there. Some came to Toronto from other parts of the country because the econ-omy was so dire. I've seen a lot of changes. Far more young people are homeless today. There is more violence. There have been quite a few attacks, including murders of homeless people.

More and more homeless people dying.

Melvin at home, 2006

I knew Eugene Upper. I used to play cards with him in the shelter. He was one of the three men who froze to death in Toronto. He died on Spadina in a bus shelter. I went to the Freezing Deaths Inquest every day, and thought something good was gonna come out of it, but I was disappointed. I was the only homeless person allowed to be an expert witness at the inquest. I wasn't scared to testify. I wanted to testify more about one of the homeless men who died, Eugene Upper, but when I was on the witness stand, they said I could only talk about my present life, not my former life or the homeless men. The Coroner and the Crown Attorney thought homelessness had nothing to do with the deaths. I wanted to say that Eugene could have been helped more. He could have had a place to live where there were housing workers on site for support and help. Workers that lived in the building or weren't too far away.

This is what I believe and what I prepared in my 1996 legal "will-say" for lawyer Peter Rosenthal, who represented the Toronto Coalition Against Homelessness:

My feeling about the men who died in the street is that they were too alone. I feel that there has to be housing so that people don't freeze in the streets. There needs to be outreach to people so that they feel that they have a friend they can trust. There needs to be non-profit housing. I believe that social housing is necessary. Premier Mike Harris plans to stop social housing. He is taking away any hope from the hundreds of Melvins out there. Harris is taking away any chance of getting off the streets and getting a place to call home. Housing in Ontario is a right, not a privilege.

They repeatedly tried to stop me from talking about housing on the witness stand. But I was able to say on the stand, "Most homeless people want housing."

Later, when the inquest was over and the jury's verdict was delivered – attributing the deaths to homelessness, I joined with the Toronto Coalition Against Homelessness and delivered the verdict to Housing Minister Al Leach's office, one block away. We were not allowed in by security guards, even to deliver the letter and the jury verdict.

> **"Victim 'could have been me' frozen man's pal tells inquest"**
>
> – Rebecca Bragg, *Toronto Star*, July 19, 1996
>
> "It could have been me who froze to death," Tipping told the inquest into the freezing deaths last winter of Upper and two other homeless men. "I slept outside many times." Although coroner Dr. Murray Naiberg disallowed questions about what his life was like while he was homeless, Tipping told the *Star* outside the hearing that he had been without housing for 14 years. Sometimes he slept in hostels but most of the time he lived on the street…. Contrary to testimony heard earlier, Upper "wanted housing quite badly and wanted to quit drinking," he said…. "Upper's dislike of hostels was understandable," Tipping said. "In hostels, people rob you, beat you up. Most homeless people want housing…."

Wenda and Melvin

I recently got in touch with Wenda to ask her about her memories of Melvin. Wenda has remained up north working for the Yukon government in the First Nations community of Pelly Crossing. She was curious about Melvin and offered these memories.

– Cathy

"I don't think that there was anything in particular that drew me to Melvin other than Melvin's persistence and my interest in wanting to help him achieve what he wanted, which was safe housing. He felt he was getting 'too old to do this anymore' and he wanted housing that he didn't have to keep moving from or be afraid to go to. That's the state he was in when I got involved in helping him. He felt that some nights it was safer to sleep in a park or a hostel instead of his rooming house. I remember feeling somewhat distraught that an older person would be in his situation.

When I met Melvin he had just started using the Street Health clinics that were held in All Saints Church. I was a nursing student doing my comprehensive placement for my degree. He was a very apologetic-looking man who talked softly, with sparkling blue eyes. He told me how he made money by delivering flyers and that he walked hours doing this. I remember that it took a few visits to get him comfortable enough to even let me look at his feet, but he did. In fact, he liked the care and came back frequently. I think it was during this time that I learned of his

Outside the minister's office I read the following to his representative, and to members of the community who were present (this was the third time the letter had been delivered to the minister's office): "We are looking to you as minister to take personal responsibility for these matters. The Coalition would like to meet with you at your earliest convenience to create a plan of action."

housing issues. It wasn't until I worked for Street Health that I was able to assist him through the paperwork and interviews that were needed for the affordable housing. I remember how nervous Melvin was about going to the meetings. We tried three times before being able to make the first appointment. I remember my frustrations at the interviews that seemed endless. I finally got upset and said that it sounded like they were not interested in giving him housing. We had travelled by subway at least four times to do these interviews and there always seemed to be something else that they needed, or another form that Melvin needed to fill out. After I spoke out we were told he had made the list and we went to view the apartment. We talked of his fears about having housing, and his past experiences, the difficulty of keeping the place clean, making the rent on time, being bored, and resorting to drinking. We dealt with his concerns one by one, at his pace and his priority, over a six-month period. For example, it was important for him to have access to a library and to be able to get phone calls and bus tickets to stay in touch with us. On moving day he was so nervous, he was unable to really participate, but he did move in!

Finding housing was a long and tedious process and the bureaucracy seemed to work against helping those it was set up to help. I remember thinking, "no wonder people give up trying." I was feeling that way at times, but I was determined not to quit as long as Melvin was holding in there.

He was really proud of his achievement. I think I was more worried about whether it would be a long-term success, but Melvin has proved that he was able to do it."

A staff person from the minister's office said it wasn't his responsibility. The meeting never happened.

I'm pretty happy with my life right now.

For the last twelve years the system has worked for me. I live in a bachelor unit. It's home, the first real one I've had since I was a child. My apartment looks like a library. I have books everywhere. I read all types of books – the last one was by Joan Collins's sister. But I read political books too. My rent just went up to $392. It's too much but it's still a bargain compared to other bachelor apartments. I'd like a larger place. I'm hoping to move into new housing, either Evangel Hall's new building, or Portland Place, around the corner from here. Ideally, I'd like a one or two bedroom.

I'm on Old Age Security and the GAINS (Guaranteed Annual Income Supplement) – that means I have a bit more money to spend now, I get about $1100 a month – but it's still hard by the end of the month.

I get some homemaking help from St. Christopher House. They clean my apartment and give me a shower twice a week – it's hard for me to reach my back. The only other thing I still need is air conditioning and a TV. The one Cathy got me broke.

Faith plays a big part in my life now. I wasn't religious as a child. I became religious when I first got the place where I live now. It happened over time. I'd almost died from a drug you take if you want to quit drinking. I drank and I had a vision that I was in hell. I was yelling, "Get me out of here!" A few friends of mine had died and I blamed God for that. One was so young. I don't blame God anymore. I was bitter for a long time. I'm not bitter anymore.

I've been in an acting group. I'm pretty good.

I don't think my life is the common story of who is homeless. I think every homeless person's story is different. Remember, there are lots of reasons why a person becomes homeless. They're not all the same. I don't think we should view homeless people as being bums. Whatever the reason they're on the street, homeless people need a place of their own.

I try to keep up with what's happening politically. I read five Toronto papers every day. I've never seen anything like the Liberal misspending that the Gomery inquiry looked into, and it makes me angry. I think Ontario is going to pay the price for the election of a Conservative government in Ottawa. We're in bad trouble now because of Stephen Harper. I think he's going to really hurt Ontario money-wise. I don't think there will be any more buildings built apart from the ones that are started. That makes me feel sad.

CHAPTER 3

DRI

URBAN LEGEND

Dri's self-portrait, 1975

I first met Dri at Tent City in the winter of 1999. He was one of the first settlers at the waterfront encampment and kept to himself – almost like a hermit. I was a bit nervous about meeting him because there were so many stories about him. He had become an urban legend.

My first impression of Dri was how gentle he seemed. He was statuesque and had a remarkable beard. But what struck me most was his soft voice and how good-natured he was even when the weather was bitter cold or raining, which made living conditions at Tent City pretty miserable.

Roughly a year later, I remember becoming alarmed when then CBC reporter Adam Vaughan warned me that the media circus around Tent City might drive Dri out. "Dri is going to leave," he asserted. "There's too much media attention. Too many people are crowding in on him."

I later learned that Dri wanted to maintain his privacy because he was concerned that his elderly parents might see him on the news and be worried.

But he didn't leave, at least not then.

Instead, slowly but surely Dri became one of the main point people around Tent City. He participated in years of strategy work with us at the Toronto Disaster Relief Committee as we hunted for a relocation site on the waterfront. For what seemed like a year of Mondays, Dri was an active member of what we called the Tent City relocation team that included architects from architectsAlliance, real estate developer David Walsh, former Toronto mayor John Sewell, and TDRC members Beric German and myself. Every Monday when I arrived at the architects' office, Dri would be standing outside, smoking a cigarette beside his bicycle. Together, we would head inside to plot our strategies. When we finally submitted our official proposal to the City of Toronto to relocate Tent City to another piece of waterfront property, utilizing architect John van Nostrand's Pro-Home prefab model, Dri's résumé was included in the inch-thick document. His talents are evident on every line of his résumé – from the letterhead, which demonstrates his graphic design talents, to his work history, to his diverse interests: "hobbies include biology, quantum physics and duplicate bridge."

Dri has been loyal and persistent, working with other activists and the media to expose the horrendous shelter conditions, and speaking out about homeless deaths. In an article titled "Close to Home" in *This Magazine*, Dri is quoted as saying, "I'm worried that we'll soon forget that shelters are really meant for emergencies, not for living in. Homeless die everywhere, in the street or in a hospital, about a hundred a year in this city. Every three and a half weeks, we have a Walkerton-scale tainted water tragedy in Toronto."

Dri became a high-profile warrior in the larger campaign, the upstream battle in Quebec City in 2001, as we fought for a National Housing program. The Quebec activists in the social housing organization Front d'action populaire en réaménagement urbain (FRAPRU) loved his charisma and his dancing. At a dinner the night before a huge rally in Quebec City, he danced a jig, and language was no barrier. He delivered a powerful speech the next morning, "We Are All We," in a blizzard outside the Chateau Laurier Hotel, where the federal-provincial-territorial housing ministers were meeting. In my opinion, "We Are All We" should be included in any compendium of famous Canadian speeches. Dri had become a national figure.

I consider Dri my co-star in the documentary film *Street Nurse*, directed by Emmy Award winner Shelley Saywell. We often do the question-and-answer period together at screenings.

Dri even shot some of the footage for that film – footage exposing shelter conditions that did not meet the United Nations standards for refugee camps. When we saw the footage, we decided to release it to the public and not wait for the movie to come out. It made the national news and created a national and local scandal. As Dri has said to me, "If we left dogs like that, the public wouldn't stand for it." Four people on the floor in a space that, according to the United Nations, one person should be in. Lights kept on all night because of the crowding. Men and women sleeping on the floor in an airless, cramped

basement room. Hacking and coughing. No pillows. Not enough washrooms…
I could go on and on. Needless to say it doesn't look like that now, and the City
was forced to improve their Shelter Standards to better reflect UN standards for
refugee camps.

Dri continues to be a colleague but I now consider him a friend as well.
He calls my mom "Mom." And, like all friends, we have occasionally asked
each other for advice.

For example, when Dri was describing some of his cold winter survival
tactics to me during our interviews, I got more and more worried because I
was planning to sleep outside at Toronto City Hall in November as part of a
National Housing Day protest. I was cold just thinking about it, and jokingly
asked if he would sleep with us neophytes that night to make sure we didn't
die. Would he share his survival tactics? Dri just laughed and said "Sweetheart,
November 21st, it won't be all that cold!"

– Cathy

I WAS BORN IN GERMANY IN 1949. MY NAME IS RAINER KARL-
August Driemeyer. I've been Dri since I was six. Of course when you're in
school you get teased. First it was "rain, dry, ha, ha, ha!" Then it got to be "dry
smear." Finally it was just Dri.

I'm an only child. Back then in Germany you didn't go to a hospital to have
a baby, you had it at home. When I was born, there wasn't even a doctor there
or a midwife. Dad's name was Reinholt and my mom's was Kathë. On the day
I was born he wrote an amazing poem called "Home" (see p.51).

Our family came to Canada when I was four. There's no little Germany in
Toronto. If you're German you had to go way down the highway to Kitchener,
Ontario. That's where I grew up.

I was a DP – a "displaced person." People would call me "DP," and I would
be the only one in my class. The first six years I went through sixteen different
schools. We moved a lot. I guess my dad had trouble getting along with people.
I don't know. We'd be living in rooms, not an apartment. He had a short fuse; he
still does. Not only was I a DP in school, I was always the new kid, so wandering

Dri as a little boy, 1951

around in the bush by myself at Tent City or up north didn't bother me because I was kind of a loner from the beginning. Once I was in high school I joined the chess club and the bridge club, I was the kicker on the football team, I was part of things. And then my parents bought a house, and suddenly we had stability.

Dad, "Opa," was an electrical and mechanical engineer with NCR, National Cash Register. He also has a split major in philosophy and psychology from Waterloo Lutheran. When I was little, Mom, "Oma," worked in a plant that made electric fences for farms and later she worked at a piano factory. I remember her always working. There were only three Driemeyers in all of Canada when we got here. Then there were six. I got married and had two kids.

I was going to be a control systems technician, and I was going to go to Mohawk College and study pneumatic control of machine systems. But somewhere along the way I realized this was what my dad wanted me to be. I really wanted to be an artist, maybe go to art college. I was good.

Still, I got a job as a welder, a union job, around 1974, and I was making good money. When I got laid off, a bunch of us decided to go to the Yukon. I wasn't grown up when I went there in my early twenties, I was young and dumb, but I sure did grow up while I was there. I hit my pace when I was twenty-five; I reached a degree of maturity when I was in the Yukon. I worked in a timber mine, which meant we used logs to keep it from caving in. It was a lead, zinc, and silver mine. The mine was about twelve hundred metres deep. I'd always wanted to see the mountains, though I never thought I'd see them from that angle. I also worked in an open pit mine. I even had a stake of my own. I really was a prospector.

Then I did some blasting for sewer lines, so I turned into an explosives expert. I have an explosives certificate for underground, surface, and construction sites. I'll never be able to leave Canada, you know! I'm an explosives expert, a political activist, and an authorized radiation worker!

I loved it in the north. The snow is white, the air is clean, you can smell the pines. But I had an injury to my left eye and had to go to Vancouver for surgery. I was using a pick without safety glasses. They popped my eyeball out and did a bunch of things to it. It was a big adjustment being back in the south. For example, I had a lot of trouble even getting on a bus, because of the closed space. I realized I'd better spend some time in the south to get used to it again.

I was on my way to PEI when I ended up in Toronto in 1983. I was thirty-four. For the first two months, I lived at the Spadina Hotel and then I moved into the Isabella. I would come around the corner to Sherbourne and Bloor for breakfast. At the time there were only twenty-two thousand people in the whole of the Yukon. I would look out my Isabella window at St. James Town, and I'm thinking, there's more people there than in the whole damn territory.

Down south, I worked in a lot of different jobs. I had a construction company. I worked for five years with Local 598 of the Cement Masons and Plasterers Union. I worked on high rises. I worked on the SkyDome as a cement mason. I think I was union rep there.

"Home"

[Written by Opa when Dri was born. Dri recites this poem in the closing moments of the film *Street Nurse*.]

Home is where you have your parents,
Home is where you do belong,
Home is where you got your talents,
Home, your shelter from the throng,
Where your mother taught you love,
Gave first thoughts into your thinking,
Where from heaven high above,
You have seen the stars blinking,
Where your father is your guide,
Always present when you need him.
Where your life is gay and bright,
Is your home you love to live in,
But just as everywhere
Things when old will have to go,
And so your home will once not be there
But in memory it will glow.

I had a company called Dri Associates, and Dri Pool and Patio. I was the Graphics Co-ordinator at the University of Waterloo. And there were times when I was paid to be an artist.

I had met Kathy by this time, who I still think is an amazing woman. She was eighteen, I was thirty-four. We were together for ten years and then we got hitched. One year later, the marriage fell apart. We'd been together for ten years and we didn't even last a year as a marriage. I don't know how that works. It happens to other people too. We had two kids together – Matthew and Terri-Lynn, fourteen months apart. When we broke up, my daughter, the youngest, was ten months old.

I did have some contact with the kids, but that fell apart. My relationship with my parents was affected too. They stayed in contact with my ex in order to stay close to their grandchildren. I don't blame them, I'm their only child, these are the only grandchildren they're going to have.

In the 1990s my life pretty well just totally collapsed. I started to collapse physically too. My back went, my legs went, my knees. I was drinking. I was in rough shape, I was pretty much lost in space.

That's partly how I ended up in Tent City.

I had spent almost six months living in a men's shelter, a large one. When you come out of that, you're not very together. I went from the shelter to Ashbridge's Bay for the weekend, which meant I lost my bunk. One of the problems with the shelter system is there is no security. Even if you were in your bunk last night they might say, "No, you weren't." And your bunk has been given to somebody else. There's just really no security at all. That insecurity goes right to your bones. It affects your whole way of thinking and your whole life.

I would go with a friend – Miki, he's a nut, down to Ashbridge's Bay, out on the point where there's this patch of spruce trees. I called it my cottage and would stay there now and then. It was a beautiful spot. I remember sitting there at night, looking towards Rochester at huge thunderclouds and watching the lightning.

Then Miki discovered an empty field on the waterfront, so we went there. I bought a piece of plastic from a hardware store, a ten-metre piece. We ended up under a tree, the plastic over us held down by rocks. That was the beginning of Tent City. It was 1999. It was really sunny that Labour Day weekend. We were trying to be discreet. If we had a little campfire it would be behind the trees so nobody could see it from the street. We were worried about getting kicked out. Eventually there were more people. People were having bonfires and you could see their shacks from the street and stuff like that. We didn't know at the time that Home Depot owned the property.

After a couple of years, we even had support services. Anishnawbe Health would give us bologna sandwiches and soup and stuff. And we had Toby and Vic from Street Survivors. They came by one Thursday night and said, "We were just at a meeting, and Home Depot is going to kick you off the property." Home Depot was under pressure from the Harris government. Their excuse to get rid of us was because the ground was toxic.

We had all basically agreed that if Home Depot came over and said, "Everybody out of the pool," we were just going to leave. There was to be no argument, no fight, because they owned the property.

But in a situation where the government was trying to – well, it's almost like Ipperwash! So Friday morning I went down to the Fred Victor Centre and used the free phone to phone everybody in the media. Not just *Eye* and *NOW*. I phoned every media I could think of – the CBC, Citytv, everybody. Well, I didn't phone the *Toronto SUN*. Other people contacted OCAP [Ontario Coalition Against Poverty] and TDRC. I mean, we were going to get evicted on Tuesday!

If Home Depot had announced, "We're going to build a store and you've gotta get off," okay, no problem. But when it's *them* [the government] throwing us out and not the owners, I wanted all the media to show up. "Come and check this out." Of course, they all wanted verification. So the media phoned the government and Home Depot to find out if this was really going to happen. Home Depot and the province decided, "Okay, we better not do this, this might be messy."

There we all are on a Tuesday morning and *nobody* showed up to evict us, but we were never told it was held off.

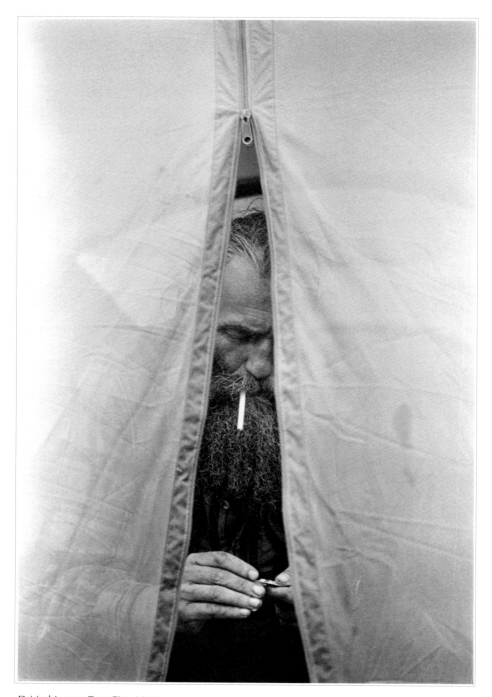

Dri in his tent, Tent City, 2000

DYING FOR A HOME

My first winter at Tent City was in one of those orange pup tents. With
–20° and –30° C, in a hoar frost, that feathery frost. In the whole inside of the
tent there would be this feathery frost and then the sun would come up on the
orange tent. It was beautiful – until it started to melt and drip on you. And the
other thing – I smoke, so there would be little particles of tar in it and if it got
in your eyes – argh!

It was cold. I had sleeping bags covering me and I bought a kerosene lamp
pretty quick. Now, when you wake in the morning you would want a drink of
water. But it's frozen solid. So, before you go to sleep, you take a jug of water
and put it underneath your parka and stick it in your armpit. When you wake
up in the morning, you've got water. And you've got another one, which is ice.
You're figuring, pretty soon this one's going to be empty. You take the one full
of ice and you stick that in your armpit. If you're wondering why you're cold,
it's because you've got this chunk of ice in your armpit! There's so many little
things about being homeless and sleeping on the street that people wouldn't
understand. If you see a guy sitting on the sidewalk and shivering, he may have
a bottle of ice tucked under his arm.

Then I moved from a tent to a lean-to.

Miki and I had a cable strung between a couple of trees, and there was plastic over it. It got real windy down there, and the wind screwed it all up. Miki
was working as a courier at the time. So, there was the odd piece of two-by-
four lying around. Using a chunk of brick and a piece of metal, I put the piece
of metal on the two-by-four and wacked it with the brick until the wood broke.
I got all the two-by-fours together and pried out some old rusty nails using
chunks of brick. Then I lined it all up, nailed this frame together, covered it
with plastic and built a lean-to for Miki. Miki said, "Wow, you're carrying altru-
ism to an infinite degree." But then I told him, "Yours is the practice one – then
I'm building one for myself." So, then I built one for myself. We stayed there
for a while.

One night Miki put some tea candles down on a box of chocolates. It
melted them, then the plastic. The plastic caught on fire and whoosh! We lost
everything in an instant. We had a third plastic shed I'd built. Using a five-

gallon pail, I'd made an airtight stove. I cut the tops and bottoms off some pop cans and wired them together to make a chimney. You use what you have. We burned chunks of two-by-four, and were nice and warm, even in the dead of winter.

One of the amazing things about Tent City is that, from the beginning, there was a sense of community. By the end there were over a hundred people living there. There was tension at times, but overall, people used a certain amount of restraint. If you went to Markham and randomly grabbed a hundred adults off the street and threw them in a fenced-in yard, it wouldn't take long before all kinds of weird things happened. Whereas with us, if you were hungry and somebody else had food, they would feed you. I mean we were in a community where a quarter is a lot of money. It was that kind of community, right from the beginning.

We had our own lingo. If you find a little cigarette butt, it's a Chevy. If you find a big butt, it's a Cadillac. If it's still burning, it's a Cadillac with the motor running. And if somebody's dashing into a movie rental place or whatever and he's got a cigarette he's ready to throw it down, but he hands it to you, that's called a limo. You know, it's like opening the door of a limo for you – handed to you.

At first I worried about publicity because of my parents. It was mostly a sense of this being my private life. I've got some problems, and I don't want the world to be involved. But I also felt a responsibility to deal with media because nobody else wanted to talk to them. I always felt that we should have contact with the media. We wanted their coverage to be positive. I felt, so it's going to inconvenience me, but so what. I don't know how others saw me. We were a totally anarchistic community. There was no leader. Although there were a few times when people would come up and say, "Dri, what are we going to do about this?"

By this point I was feeling healthier. I felt better once I'd moved into Tent City. But there was no sense of security there either. Every time you came down Parliament Street and round the corner, you're looking to see if bulldozers have

Dri and burnt-out tent, Tent City, 2000

flattened it. There was a certain degree of that. You don't have a key, you don't have a lease. But still there was a sense of community and a feeling that maybe they were going to leave us alone.

So then I went from a lean-to to a little house.

TDRC put in two duplexes called DuraKits. Somehow it got decided that I would move in to one. It had a front door with a lock, although I tried the key in the door and it broke. So here I am where I have a door but only half a key. The other half is in the lock but it's broken. A door with a lock. Wow – but that's okay. Most of us just kind of had a tent flap. The lean-to just had a flap. I was in a duplex house, next to Chris. I miss him!

I thought the DuraKits were neat. First of all, it's a cardboard thing. If you get mad enough, you can put your fist through it anywhere, but it kept the bugs out.

There was quite an effort by TDRC to relocate us into legitimate housing for the long-term. Part of that team was John van Nostrand from architectsAlliance. They do a lot of work all over the world. He really does have an interest in housing. And that level of housing. He's designed structures with very few two-by-fours and very few nails. You can actually design something you can sleep in and then add to it later. Of course, our by-laws here wouldn't allow that. But they do it in Mongolia and other places. He goes out there to promote these projects.

We had a lot of meetings at the offices of architectsAlliance with John and Jon, the architects, John Sewell, always David Walsh, John Andras, Karl and Patrick and me representing Tent City, and Beric German, Danielle Koyama, and Cathy. It was a very positive experience. We met in a room with a burnished steel table. Much of our energy went into finding another piece of land to move Tent City to. The agenda was basically to put an RFP [Request for Funding Proposal for the City] together – in fact, my bio is in the RFP with my logo. We had even established a lot of the financing ourselves. But first we had to find a location. We went out with Jack Layton and John van Nostrand late at night, all around the waterfront looking for a piece of property. The property we picked was a TEDCO property at 525 Commissioners Street. And it turned out that many of the TEDCO properties in that vicinity were up in the air because Toronto's Harbour Commission was in the process of going through the courts to find out who actually owned the land. All that effort came to naught.

And then the eviction.

A few weeks before we were evicted from Tent City, my friend Hazel saw my parents walk by. She looked at them and said, "You guys aren't Dri's parents by any chance, are you?" And neither one of them had a beard! They had seen me on TV, had come to Toronto, and found Tent City. They left a message on my door. Soon after that, the eviction occurred. All of a sudden the police and security guards arrived – real jerks – and bang, it was gone. I couldn't even get my bicycle. I got nothing out of the place. It was like, "No, get out now!"

Media scrumming Dri, Tent City eviction, 2002

I knew the day would come eventually, but for it to be like that! I could see them saying, "You guys got to be out by next Thursday." Or something like that to give us a chance to get our stuff together. I couldn't imagine *why* they did it like that. I remember a picture in the newspaper, *Eye* or *NOW*, of two girls hugging, comforting each other, a black girl and a white girl. It was such a gorgeous picture. The emotions on their faces as they were holding each other captured the feelings of that day. I remember that more than anything else about the day.

We all ended up at Woodgreen Community Centre. I slept in the park across the street. I wasn't going to sleep in a gym full of people. That's like going back to the hostels and the Out of the Cold programs. I was there for a week or two, and within forty-eight hours of the eviction a special Rent Supplement program was announced to help us afford rents. This program came from federal money that was just sitting there, unspent, at the provincial level; the

City runs the program. I found an apartment in Parkdale. I've been there ever since. I like the location.

This is the first time I've been well housed in fifteen years. I'm still getting used to flushing the toilet. I still have a tent – in my bedroom. I don't have curtains, but I figure if I'm in a tent people won't see me.

I'm on ODSP [Ontario Disability Support Program] and have about $500 left for spending money after I pay my rent. My rent in total is $900. So part of my cheque goes to rent and the rent supplement covers the rest. The only problem is the monies go to private landlords. The city should be going out and buying housing. Housing, housing, housing – we need it all over the city. In the end, I think what we have, the rent supplement program, is better than having all of us in one place. Now the government has even announced another two hundred rent supplements because our Tent City program worked so well.

And there's still federal money just sitting there!

A lot of the things I did through TDRC in the last few years led me to end up in offices like the architects' where I'm listened to with a certain amount of respect. It's pleasant.

Over the years, I've done a lot of media, from many angles. I shot the secret video of the shelter conditions for the Shelley Saywell film *Street Nurse*. Can you imagine if I'd been caught? I would have been in trouble, but the images had to be captured on film. It was so bad in there. The next day it was on the front page of the *Toronto Star*. In my new place, I've done a few TV interviews.

I do a lot of public speaking now to journalism students, to nursing and social work students, at high schools. Now, they are *so receptive*. They get it. I think they get it better than their teachers. I think I've done some great speeches.

I've just joined the Steering Committee for the Toronto Disaster Relief Committee. I felt quite honoured to be asked. I'm not sure if I've really contributed all

Speech by Dri at Quebec City, 2001

We are all we.

We need to convince the other we,

That we need help.

We need housing. We need housing.

Merci!

that much, but I've just started. "I haven't sold a car yet!" It's like being a used car salesman. "Haven't sold a car yet." I feel proud to be with these people. I presented to the Ontario pre-budget committee recently at the InterContinental Hotel with Michael Shapcott. When we finished I told them to sign the cheque. I'll speak anywhere, anytime. I may not be great, but probably whatever I do, I won't be half bad. I can make my point in one minute.

I've had quite an eventful year. I had promised Oma and Opa that I would spend Christmas with the whole family in Waterloo. So, having made that promise, and committed myself, I went there for Christmas with my ex and the kids and we all had Christmas dinner together. It went as well as I'd expected it to; it went really well actually. I don't hide any of the Tent City stuff from them. Basically, poverty and homelessness isn't something you should be embarrassed about.

In fact, I've been back a lot since. It's been quite an experience. When I show up my ex can go out and then I'm stuck in a townhouse full of teenagers! Matthew has just turned seventeen and Terri-Lynn just turned sixteen. They're good kids, they're helpful kids, they're great. I enjoy their company. I go to Galt a couple times a month to see them. Kathy, my ex, runs something like a drop-in centre in her house for the kids and their friends. It's amazing. It's like Tent City. Welcome to reality. It's as real as it gets. Sometimes there are a lot there, and Kathy looks after them. Some of my kids' friends remember me. When they were little, I used to bring the blankets out, and the chairs, and drape the blankets over the chairs, like a tent. Then I would bring out lemonade or iced tea in a little tea set with crackers or biscuits. How many fathers do that? These kids say, "I remember him!"

Then Opa died. He fell down a flight of stairs at home and died without regaining consciousness, with Oma beside him.

The other thing that's changed for me is I had a stroke. On February 14th, Valentine's Day – such a heartthrob! I woke up not being able to move things, and at first I thought I'd pinched a nerve. Then I started to realize that my right leg was dead too and everything else. So it was about four days before I ended up at the hospital and they said, "You had a stroke and it took you four days to come in?" "Well, I don't go to doctors all that often." They did the MRIs and everything within a week.

My progress has been good. My ex-wife is a physiotherapist, so she gives me advice like "keep doing what you're doing, just keep using it."

At first it was really strange. Try putting toothpaste on a toothbrush with one hand. Try using a can opener with one hand. Try doing just about anything. Take your predominant hand, your right hand like me, and duct tape it behind your back. Then you know. Or just duct tape a splint to it and all the fingers so you can't really move anything. It's just a club. You really don't understand until it happens, how important your body is.

I have been quite emotional in the last little while. Last week I showed *Street Nurse* at the National Homelessness Conference, and it was the first time I'd seen it in a long, long time. I burst into tears. I don't know why; it's one of the mental phases I go through. All the difficulties that I had before haven't been replaced by this stroke. There was a certain amount of emotional instability, and you know that's basically still all there, and now I've got the stroke on top of it. And even the depression, a lot of it is still there. I mean, the situation has been alleviated to a certain extent by being housed and reunited with the family, but, I don't know, it's hard to explain.

Prose by Dri

The cold.........cold........

..........world of white

He struggles though the cold, cold world of blowing snow.

The world of blowing.........

.........blowing..........swirling........

..........white

Cold and bright.........the swirling white.........

...........cold..........

The Neolithic hunter struggles and

stumbles in his quest.........

..........he falls into the bed of

white.........

..........he struggles to his feet again

to fight his

way through the world of

blowing..........swirling........

white

.........but knows not why.........

His mate has surrendered herself to the cold

blowing world of white.........cold........

.........cold.........blowing.........world........

..........of..........

.........his two children.........

.............gone..........

...........lost to the

cold world of swirling white.........

.........children..........

.............children..........

...........he loved and wanted........

..........lost..........

..........lost to the cold.........the unending cold

..........lost to the cold.............the unending cold

clear world of white..........

His spear drops from frozen fingers into

a bright.........blinding..........swirling world of white

....

.............cold..........swirling world

...........of white

He must go on.........

.........on to the sea

The wondrous sea.........

the sea will be

his salvation.........

The sea will provide food to nourish him

.........food in the cold.........cold

..........world of bright white

He stumbles again..........

....

tries to rise.........

.........rise up into a world of white.........

.........he tries to rise.........

.........He tries to rise.........he must find

the sea.........

....

....

....

He awakens.........it's another

nightmare.........

.........He lies in his sleeping bag

on the cold, cold..........cold.........concrete.........

..........under a piece of plastic blowing

in the winter wind..........

..........his mate..........

and beloved children are a memory

of a long time ago and very bitter divorce

..........long time ago.........bitter.........

..........the bitter swirling.........

............cold.........

..........the whirling world of

blowing white swirls about him and

his torn tarp as he shudders

and trembles in a cold.........cold..........

..........world of white

.........Maybe tonight the cold will claim him.........

..........maybe tonight the torment will end.........

..........end in the cold..........

..........white..........

..............maybe tonight he

will find ....

..........eternal peace..........

....

– by Rainer (DRI) Driemeyer

NANCY BAKER

WITNESS TO ALL

Nancy decorating her trailer, Christmas, 2000

I first met Nancy in the drop-in at All Saints Church at Sherbourne and Dundas. It would have been around 1989, when I was working at Street Health.

I thought she had the kind of face that photographers would love – soft and expressive, with crinkly little laugh lines around her eyes. I still think so. I remember her face being always tanned from spending so much time outside. Her face is more weathered today. Nancy has earned just about every line on her face. She's spent most of the years I've known her in and out of shelters, and "out" means living right outside. She survives, but many of her peers have not.

More than anyone I know, she's lost a lot of people. I remember going with Nancy to visit her partner Jeff when he was in St. Mike's ICU. They were both so young, and he had just been diagnosed with a faulty heart valve. He died not long after. Since then Nancy has lost other loved ones, most recently partner Steve, to cancer. She knows most of the names on the Homeless Memorial Board in downtown Toronto.

As Nellie McClung proclaimed, "First mourn. Then organize." Nancy, perhaps more than anybody else who has witnessed the extent of the deaths over the years, has really allowed herself to fold into the grief and the loss. Yet, in her own way, she continues to come out fighting. She is considered feisty on the streets, rebellious at City Hall, and she's been fighting on the homeless front for many years.

I once asked Nancy what she thought I should say in my next speech. She said, "Tell the people that we are dying. People are dying for a home."
– Cathy

I WAS BORN IN BRANTFORD, ONTARIO, IN 1959. ONE OF MY FIRST memories is living above a TV repair shop. A fire started in the shop and I was rescued and carried out by one of the firemen, in his jacket.

When I was three we moved. My dad was a truck driver, originally from Nova Scotia. He did long hauls and was away for long periods. Where my dad got work is where we lived. We were bounced all over – to Hamilton, Caledonia, Stoney Creek.

I was the oldest of eight. Mostly, my mom tried to rent a house instead of an apartment. Houses had more room. School was a problem. Some of us went to the Catholic schools, some the Protestant. I was brought up both. I hated all the rules and skipped school a lot. I only went to Grade 7 but I've been tested and have about a Grade 5 education.

When I was about twelve I wanted to leave home. I was the oldest, and if my mom and dad went out I was always the babysitter for five brothers and two sisters. My dad drank a lot. When he was home there was usually arguing, fighting, drinking. A lot of fighting with my mom. So I went to live with my grandparents in Brantford. After a year at my grandparents my parents wanted me to come home. They said, "We'll change everything." First it was quiet back at home, then the fighting started all over again.

I ran away all the time. I was always getting caught. There was this one detective named Sergeant Clue – I used to call him "Sergeant Clueless."

Growing up I didn't have many friends. I didn't like being around big groups. I had a part-time job after school at a variety store. The old guy who owned it was pretty good. I needed a pair of glasses and he went out and bought my glasses. My dad was on the road at Christmas that year, and the old guy had my mom and all of us kids over for Christmas and put on a big meal. He was a really nice guy. Once I was put in a group home – like an observation home, until I went to court for being a runaway.

Then I ran away again! I was almost fourteen. I ran off with the man who ended up being my husband. I got pregnant and we were married just before my fifteenth birthday. My dad said, "You get her pregnant, you marry her." When I was pregnant my ex threw me down three flights of stairs. I left. My baby, a girl, was born on December 13th, 1974, and I lived with my mom. But then, I ended up back together with my ex and we had another baby girl two years later, but the marriage didn't last long. I was pretty much on my own from the time my oldest was born. My mom helped raise my youngest.

My mom and the girls are still in Hamilton and I have three grandchildren now. They don't like the fact that I live in Toronto.

My experiences with abuse did prepare me to work in a pilot project at Regent Park Community Health Centre in downtown Toronto. I was an out-reach worker there for six months. I would meet with women one-on-one and help them to find shelter or a safe house. It was kind of frustrating – when you know what you've been through and you're trying to deal with someone who may not want to leave home, but is still in an abusive situation. But I liked the work. In fact, later I tried to enroll at George Brown College so I could get involved in the shelter system, but they said I didn't have the proper schooling level. Actually I've been thinking about going back to school for upgrading and going into the same field. I'm good in English. When I took an English corres-pondence course I got 98 percent.

After Jeff died I went to Saskatoon to stay with my brother. While I was there my dad died in Hamilton, and when I came back to Toronto for his funeral I had lost my apartment. I stayed at just about every women's shelter, many times. It was very stressful. I was attacked in a women's shelter. I know that the woman that attacked me was ill, so rather than have the shelter kick her out, I said I'd leave.

Once in a while I would rent a hotel room for one or two nights at the Gladstone or the Budget, just to get out of the shelter system. Lots of people do that, just to get a rest. It used to cost $20–$25 a night. Sometimes I slept outside a lot, like on a grate (I still have a steam burn from the grate), or sometimes on cardboard laid out on park benches, or the gazebo at St. James Park. The gazebo there meant we could stay dry if it rained. When the police began harassing us to kick us out, a friend said to me, "There's a place, a vacant lot on the water. You can build a hut there." I went down and that's where I stayed for five years – Tent City. There were three others already there – Gord, Dri, and Miki. I was the first girl at Tent City. I felt very comfortable, I never had a problem. I stayed in a gutted-out van that was already there. It was stripped, no windows, and it had no floor. I installed styrofoam where the empty windows were. I draped sleeping bags over it for insulation.

While I was living outside, I was receiving about $485 – the "living allow-ance" – from ODSP because I have some long-term health problems. But after you buy your heavy clothing, you still need more. So over the years I have nearly always "panned" at Bay and Dundas. That's been the corner I've been at for seven years. I started panning when I was at Tent City because some of the food banks didn't want to give us food because we "didn't have an address."

Early on, we were threatened with eviction by the City and the Province, due to the fact that the land was contaminated. Home Depot owned the land and wanted to put a big-box store on the property, on contaminated land! Well, I've got some thoughts on that. We had no warnings; just the written notices left on our door, and we knew what those notices meant. These guys are threat-ening to throw us out and where were we gonna go? I helped to organize a demonstration – we weren't going to let them push us out. So, I made the calls to OCAP because I knew Gaetan, and I called TDRC, because I knew Cathy and Beric. We held a press conference in the pouring rain at Tent City on the day of the eviction.

Well, they backed off! And we just continued to live there for a few more years.

A few more people came, including my friend Marty. For a while, we were thirteen and we all stayed together. Marty and I moved into a camper that was donated to us by a guy from Calgary who had gotten a new one. He just showed up one day in his truck and asked if anyone would like his old camper on the back of his truck, and we lifted it off.

The camper was a little crowded for two people. But we managed. We didn't put any furniture in it. It already had a three-quarter size bed. It had a sink, but we had to keep a bucket underneath it. It even had wiring but we didn't trust it. Even before the generators arrived, it was warm enough for two people. We had extra blankets, and we sealed off and winterized it. We bought glue, duct tape, and tarp, and did the windows to keep out the cold air.

Nancy in her trailer with friend Duane, Tent City, 2000

Other people then were living in little shacks, or makeshift shelters, or tents. We all kind of pitched in to help each other. We started getting propane and used it to fuel small heaters. One year TDRC helped us get a generator that ran on diesel. Our clothes always smelled from the fuel or from sitting around the fire barrel. Once I went into the Health Centre and one of the workers went running all over looking for the fire.

Later I moved into one of the little DuraKits. They were like little doll-houses. TDRC brought them down and there was a draw to see who would live in them. Cathy pulled the winning name out of the "hat" and Glenda won, but Glenda gave the prize to me. Eventually I moved into the big house that was brought down. We called it "the palace"! It was really called a Pro-Home and was a step-up from a DuraKit. I called it home. It was a two hundred square foot house, it came all furnished, you had your own cupboards, a sink, and you had a shower, and they were going to install a composting toilet. Before that the DuraKit was home. I used to call it the "Little House on the Prairie."

We had our routines. The ducks we called Donald and Daisy would quack at us and we would wake up early. Then we would gather kindling for the fire barrel, start the fire barrel, put the kettle on, make coffee, sit around the fire barrel, go collect water, boil it, do dishes, and do laundry. We did our laundry in five gallon pails by hand, and hung it on a clothesline. Sometimes we would take our laundry up to the Health Centre. During the day, most people left for various things – errands, appointments, to see friends. In bad weather – when it rained or when it was really cold – we would all go up to the drop-in at All Saints Church.

We even had a water source, until Mayor Mel Lastman shut it off. He had come down and been driven through on a tour and next thing we knew it was shut off. Jack Layton convinced the City to turn the water back on.

We all shared stuff down there, even food. Someone would make a big pot of Beefaroni or something and share it. It was home. Better than a park bench. I felt hopeful, but then the police would come down and warn us we were going to be kicked off, "Don't make yourself comfortable," they'd snarl. I just thought – oh, here we go again.

Nancy to Minister Bradshaw

Nancy sat politely for me one winter's day, wearing a vest and a red and white toque. Working with filmmaker Michael Connolly, I asked her to speak to the camera, directly to the Minister Responsible for Homelessness, Claudette Bradshaw. I promised Nancy I would deliver her message. Totally unrehearsed, she gave a stellar performance:

Dear Claudette Bradshaw,

My name is Nancy Baker, and I'm a resident of Tent City. I've been down there approximately two years. Minister Bradshaw, we're coming to you on behalf of us homeless people. Please give us housing. Help us in this disaster where we are. If we had affordable housing, if we had suitable housing, and not shelters, there wouldn't be as many people dying on the streets as there is today.

As we grew to forty and then to sixty people, we began having a lot of community meetings with the TDRC. They would bring down Kentucky Fried Chicken for dinner and then we would have our meeting outside around a big round table. There was often a lot of conflict and built-up anger that came out at those meetings. Beric usually chaired them and a few of us would try to help things stay smooth. People had their own point of view. Some people thought the meetings would create more problems. There was often jealousy over who got what. Discussions turned into gripes. Usually a meeting would be called when there was already a problem, like the maintenance of the portable toilets, or when a problem was anticipated, such as another eviction threat. We were always worried, never knowing when the eviction would happen.

There were times when TDRC would bring outside help in on the weekends. Unions like CUPE and CAW and university students and church volunteers would come and help with work parties, like the winter insulation day or the clean-up days. During the garbage strike, contractors from outside were dumping big time and we ended up with rats. We had fun on the work party days – we would even be joined by young people from religious groups in the United States. Most of us would join in and help in the clean-up. I enjoyed the work parties because then people could see we were trying to keep the place clean. We would also have a big meal together catered by a drop-in centre like PARC or en Ville catering, and the meal would be like a family gathering, like a reunion.

In fact, we had a lot of outside help. Street Survivors brought us candles and blankets. Street nurses came down with first aid supplies. Cathy and TDRC brought in the toilets. David Walsh, the propane. Barry Burnett, a construction contractor from Buttcon Ltd., helped raise money and install the wood stoves. Project Warmth helped pay for a lot of this.

At one point we even had our own gardens. We had boxes above ground and soil was brought in and we planted tomatoes. We kind of fended for ourselves for our fresh vegetables. A lot of us really got into planting.

Marty and I used to get up pretty early. The wildlife was always there. The ducks would quack at us when it was their feeding time. We had this duck we used to call Daisy that would squawk at us in the morning, right through the van, if we didn't get up. That was a really nasty article the *Toronto SUN* printed saying we were killing the squirrels and eating them. It wasn't true. I wrote a letter to the editor, which they printed.

During Toronto's Olympic bid, when the IOC [International Olympic Committee] and all the media were in town, sometimes you couldn't move down at Tent City. It was like a big media circus because where we were was supposed to be the site of the Athletes' Village. On the day of the Olympic decision we were down on Cherry Street for a big breakfast, watching the decision on a TV run on a generator. Toronto lost. We kind of lost too. Because after that I think they decided they were just gonna come in full force and put more pressure on us to leave the property – to force us out. There was never a guarantee for how long we could last on the site.

I was part of the City Hall meetings with Jack Layton when we worked together to try to save or relocate Tent City somewhere else on the waterfront. At night, we would all go looking at other sites like Cherry Beach to move to. Jack was always going to bat for us saying, "These people need housing." He had conversations with Home Depot. I think that's why we were allowed to stay there as long as we did. But a lot of City Council didn't want us there, and Jack would say to them, "What are you going to do with them? You haven't given them housing!"

We had put in a bid for a site on Commissioners Street with TDRC, the architectsAlliance, and Woodgreen Community Centre. I thought that was going to be all right for us. The new site would have been safe, with some Pro-Home houses, including one with a meeting room hooked up to the grid with

> **Letter to the Editor, *Toronto SUN*, July 18, 2001**
>
> I have been a resident of Tent City for the last two years. I have never killed an animal. I feed the animals – geese, ducks, and squirrels come and eat right out of my hand. We have named the animals. We call the ducks Daisy and Donald, and the geese Fred and Wilma. What you published in *The SUN* about us eating animals is just not true. Just because we are homeless doesn't mean we are cruel to animals.
>
> – Nancy Baker, Tent City, Toronto

Unsigned eviction notice left by authorities at Tent City, 2000

electricity, showers, toilets, and running water. If we'd been allowed to relocate it would have been great. But we lost to another group – Homes First, and nothing has happened since on either property, except the eviction.

The day of the eviction was pretty discouraging actually. I was on my way up town when I ran into my friend Penny, from Tent City, who said "You'd better get down to Tent City. They're evicting everybody. There's police, security, everything." I never got back in. So, I ended up losing everything. The Pro-Home. All my clothes, I lost everything. A lot of things I can't replace. Pictures of my kids. Pictures of my boyfriend Steve. But the most precious thing I lost was my freedom.

Everybody was up in arms because no one knew what was going to happen to us. People with pets, where were they gonna go?

I know from the media's point of view that we were homeless. They actually called us a shantytown. I knew I was homeless, but I also knew that I

Nancy at Tent City, 2000

wasn't sleeping on a park bench, or on the sidewalk. I had a roof over my head at Tent City.

I hear now that they are planning a movie called *Love on the Waterfront*. Maybe it's based on Shaughnessy Bishop-Stall's book *Down to This*. I refuse to read it. He lived with us at Tent City, presenting himself as one of us. We didn't know he was writing a book about us at the time. I would want Sally Field to play me because she was so feisty in Norma Rae!

Then I got into the Tent City rent supplement program. Steve and I first shared a place before he got sick with cancer. He was in and out of hospital and he did not get good care before he died.

I've got a one bedroom apartment now through the Tent City housing pilot. I'm still not used to being on my own, but Marty lives in the same building now, so that's good. If it wasn't for the rent supplement program, I wouldn't be able to afford a place. I'm on ODSP and get $863 a month. The average rent in Toronto for a one bedroom is $800. The average waiting list for a subsidized unit in Toronto is twelve years.

So, in this program I pay $139 and my rent is topped up with the rent supplement. I've just recently had to move because my other place was on the fourth floor, and it was too hard because of my injuries. I was assaulted a couple of years ago and ended up with a badly broken leg, so I needed a ground floor apartment. It's great, but it's boiling – no air conditioning, and this summer we had this killer heat wave. Some day I'd like a balcony. After living at Tent City I hate being closed in.

I'm going shopping this afternoon. I have to buy a mop and pail. Also, some meat and potatoes. I'm not much of a vegetable eater. A special treat would be to cook ribs. I just got some books second-hand from the church: *From Canada's Southernmost Kitchens Cookbook*, and Grisham's *The Runaway Jury*.

I'm happy to have an apartment now because I have seen things get so much worse. There are more people out there now. There are more couples. There is more violence in the shelters than I have ever seen. People are getting stressed out. The shelters are overcrowded – I mean with a few hundred people in some of them. I've heard that some people can't keep their jobs once they hit the shelters because they have to be in by curfew.

I've survived a lot of people's deaths. Another friend of mine, Barb, died a couple of days ago. They found her dead in her apartment. Barb used to stay at Tent City. Yesterday I found out that a woman, who used to sleep at City Hall with a lot of stuffed toys, died. She was my neighbour when I slept at City Hall. An older man sleeping in his sleeping bag was beaten to death. He was murdered! Three army reservists were charged with first-degree murder. They're all senseless deaths. I go to the Homeless Memorial every month and I often speak out because the government should be doing more. Just because I'm housed, well, there are a lot of people still out there. A lot have died; I know most of the names on the Memorial Board.

I've done some art over the years, at the Adelaide Women's Resource Centre, and some of my work has been exhibited at City Hall. I made a house, and wrote on it, "Everyone needs a home." I don't really see any progress. I've lost trust in all the politicians. I can show my painting inside City Hall, but then they've made it illegal for me, if I was still homeless, to sleep outside there. I don't think that's right. The City is planning a "needs assessment," but, as far as I'm concerned, it's really a count, and I bet there will be hundreds of people not counted because the volunteers won't know how to find them.

Things are bad all over for people. Now you can barely find an agency that will give you food or a sleeping bag, because the City has put a stop to it. If you're in a park or even on a park bench around the church here, the police or the Parks guys make you leave. I got a ticket recently for "encovering the sidewalk" – for taking too much space on the sidewalk.

We have to keep raising public awareness to get the government to do something. That's what we've been doing for years. At least now they're promising money for housing. It's pretty discouraging though because we've not seen a penny of it. Just because I'm housed doesn't mean I'll stop fighting for the homeless. How many people are going to die because our government won't build affordable housing?

CHAPTER 5

MARTY LANG

TENT CITY LEADER

Marty hauling wood, Tent City, 2000

Marty is just one really nice guy. His entire life could and should be a book because he has witnessed so much. We've known each other for twenty-one years and have developed an easygoing relationship. When he's teasing me he calls me "Crowe."

I spent more time interviewing Marty than I did anyone else in this book. He kept calling to update me on his latest news. Life kept opening doors for Marty, or Marty kept opening them. That meant eating a lot of bacon and eggs at the Ontario Restaurant – an old haunt of mine from my early days as a street nurse. At the Ontario, with a tape recorder on the table, Marty, who I would normally describe as shy, would pour his heart out, sharing stories and showing me pictures and news clippings. Stories of the Tent City eviction, more recent struggles in rental housing, rekindling family relationships, getting baptized, preparing for his next speech. There were also times when the tape recorder had to be shut off, and we wondered if the young waitress would be shocked by our tears.

If you were to meet Marty you would understand, in ways that words can't express, why everyone should have the opportunity to live in decent housing.

Today he's one of our main housing advocates, always willing to speak to groups of students, academic researchers, even the press. He's handsome, articulate, and trustworthy. He also reminds me of the sincere World War II veterans who arrived home from overseas to find no possibility for a home. They protested the housing shortage, wearing their ties and overcoats, bringing their wives and children, and took over government buildings and old hotels as temporary living quarters. What came across was their pride and their indignation at the shocking lack of housing. Their efforts led to the 1954 National Housing Act, and postwar housing that is still standing to this day.

Marty is cut from the same cloth as these early rebels. Not only has he seen a lot over at least a dozen years of homelessness, he too has acted. He engaged in life at Tent City as a true community leader, always the reliable one who could be entrusted to run the generator, always the guy presenting new ideas to us and giving us an update on problems that needed solving. He has evolved from a practical, down-to-earth guy with a personal interest in the housing issue, to an eloquent spokesman for housing rights for all.

– Cathy

MY NAME IS MARTY LANG AND I'M A COUPLE YEARS YOUNGER than the author of this book. I was the thirteenth person to move into Tent City. It was the Canada Day weekend in 1998. We were evicted in 2002, four years and two months later.

Before I moved to Tent City I'd been living in a rooming house. After I'd paid my rent I had $70 a month to live on. There was no sense locking my door because if you pushed on any door it would just open. There was no safety factor. So my friend Nancy finally talked me into moving to Tent City. She'd been there for more than a year. I knew six or seven of the other people there, and I felt extremely comfortable about the move.

We started off in an abandoned old Volkswagen van that was up on blocks and had no floor except for the one we built. The first winter we wrapped ourselves in sleeping bags to stay warm. We had so many of them piled on us that we couldn't turn over sometimes from the weight. Wild animals would come up and get into our food, especially the groundhogs. There were two foxes there at the beginning and two coyotes. If you were up very early, that's when you'd see them – they were pretty skittish. If we were slow getting up, ducks would come quacking at our door. We'd feed them stale bread. Because there were so few of us there wasn't a rat problem. The rats came later.

Tent City didn't grow much during my first winter. We were a small group on the east end. My friend Heartbeat moved down, battling stomach cancer. Brian and Karen moved down. We had our first pregnancy that winter. Because the nearest payphone was twenty minutes away down at the Cherry Beach restaurant, a nurse gave me some computer printouts and a two-hour crash course on how to deliver a baby.

Those were the pre-outhouse days when we used a human litter box behind a dumpster. We took turns hauling in fresh dirt. We were about eighteen people then and we were all living in tents and lean-tos made with tarps and stuff like that. There was no tension at that point. We were a very small group of people and there was lots of land – twenty-nine acres. No one built right on top of another person. The tension came as we grew.

Marty (second from left) with his brothers and sister, 1964

Even the next year, my second, we didn't grow that much. We were up to maybe thirty people. That winter some prefab shacks were brought down by the Toronto Disaster Relief Committee. That was the winter when we had two generators – the luxury winter. We had power and heaters, even a little black and white TV, and we joined the world. The TDRC got us two portable toilets, plenty at the time. There was one hose for running water (but it was cold!) and eventually a shower was built. Later, TDRC gave us individual solar shower bags.

I ran the generator for the east end and Patrick ran the one for the west end. We used diesel fuel. You had to pump it up every day. We were asked to use the generators only between 5 P.M. and 9 A.M. because it was so expensive. It cost $600 a month to fill each tank. The TDRC, some Rotary Club members, and Buttcon, a construction company, helped to cover the costs. During the day people could sit by the fire that was burning in an old oil drum, or by a small bonfire, to get warm. When you went into the city, everyone knew you lived at Tent City because you smelled like wood smoke all the time. In the late afternoon people would be waiting for me to get back with the key to the generator. If I was back too much after five in the afternoon they'd say, "My favourite show comes on at five, you know." As it turned out, that was the only winter we had the generators.

Once the prefab houses arrived we became kind of media darlings. When the first one was brought in there were, I think, a hundred reporters from Canada, some from Germany, the U.K., Europe, and Australia, and so all of a sudden we were mainstream news.

This first media blitz didn't affect us too much. But when even more media began to cover our battle for permanent land on the waterfront – where we would have all the amenities like hydro, then more homeless people started coming down to check Tent City out. And many of them moved in. That was okay because at that point, anyone who moved in knew at least one of the residents. There was a lot of land, and no one built on top of another person. People were starting to build houses by then. Some of the movie studios in the east end would have walls and roofs left over from their shoots and they'd donate them to Tent City. The carpenters and grips, they'd bring them down piecemeal on a flatbed truck – four walls and a ceiling. They'd just knock the nails halfway out, bring them down, and knock them back together for us.

The group that came in the fall built way off to the northeast. We called it "the swamp" because it was lowland. They would say that no one would see them down there. I happened to mention to them that they really weren't gonna like it there in the spring. And they said, "Why?" and I said, "Well, because this is the swamp, there are a million mosquitoes down there." They said, "We'll be able to handle it." They moved to higher ground that spring.

At that point Nancy and I were in the camper that had been donated by a construction worker. He said that people had been telling him all summer where Tent City was, and he took the Gardiner Expressway every day and couldn't see the tents or houses because the trees were so tall. Then, in the fall, he could see us. So he came down and offered us the camper. Everyone helped lift it off his truck and put it down. That was great. All of a sudden we were airtight. Lighting one tea candle could raise the temperature one degree Celsius in an airtight space.

On a typical day you'd wake up and psych yourself to go use the outhouse, hoping someone had used it right before you so the seat was warm. Whoever was up earliest would get the fire going. Everyone would bring over their pot of water to boil and have coffee, and you'd plan your day. Most of us were gone during the day, off panhandling, or we had appointments or whatever. A few people might stay behind and sit by the fire barrel.

Up to the first seventy-five residents, we still had a sense of community. I think most of us at Tent City felt we had a home and weren't homeless. People kept the area around each of their houses looking neat. There were garbage piles because we didn't have garbage pickup down there, but we burned most of the dry garbage. Most of the insides of the houses were kept pretty clean. During the garbage strike, people would come down and dump their garbage and construction waste at Tent City because the dumps were closed and we were just off the highway. That's when the rat problem began.

We used to have community meetings with TDRC down at Tent City. The agenda would start with whatever progress had occurred, and we'd be brought up to date on the chances of our getting new land. Then we'd usually stop and have a meal of KFC. After dinner we'd have an open meeting to talk about problems, like the need to make sure we all shared food when it was donated or to make sure we were safe around fires. Sometimes the younger folks would go a bit overboard with their campfires, and some of us older ones would have to talk to them.

Eventually I lived in a very special house in Tent City. It was built for a housing conference where TDRC and the architectsAlliance were hoping to convince churches and other organizations to put these prefab houses right on their property. The house cost about $12,000 to build, all inclusive! None of the churches wanted it, so they brought it down to us. It was gorgeous. Four inches of insulation, a wood stove, furnished right down to the knives and forks and spoons. It was called a Pro-Home, and we thought that if we ever made it to the Promised Land – that's what we called one of the sites we were looking at on the waterfront – everyone would have a Pro-Home with its own septic tank, running water, and all. It would have been perfect. That was the long-term plan.

Quite early on, around 1999–2000, around the same time that Toronto was trying to win the Olympics bid, I was part of negotiations with TDRC and the City to try to relocate Tent City, and we lost a big vote at City Hall.

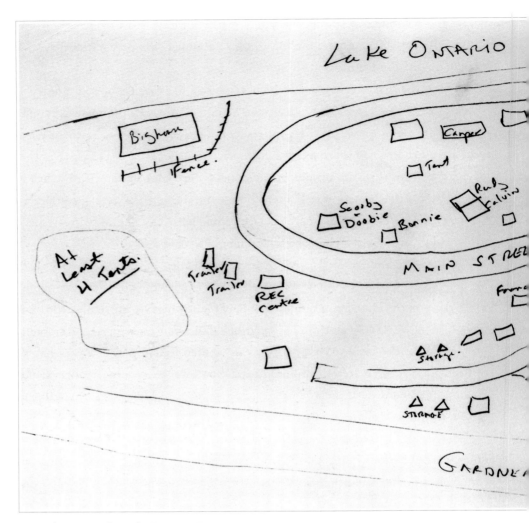

Map of Tent City, drawn by Marty, 2004

By then, both my parents were gone and I began to talk more. Up 'til then I'd been holding a lot in. There were lots of things I wanted to say, but I didn't have an outlet.

I'd had mixed feelings about the media. At first I didn't want to talk to them. When my parents were still alive, they wouldn't have understood. Most

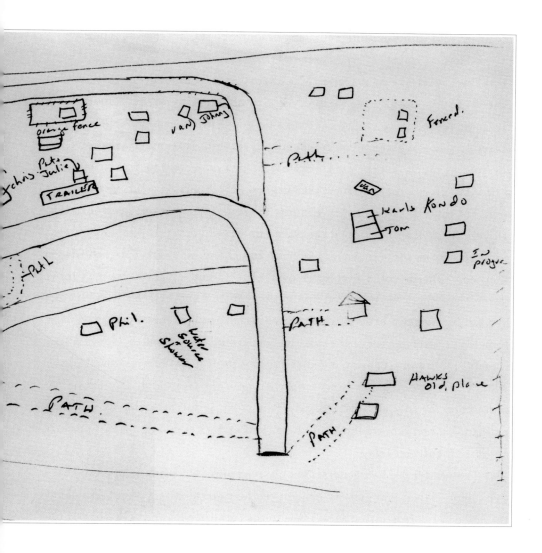

of the media respected my wish to not go on camera. When Citytv did the five-part series on Tent City, I was one of the people featured in it, but Adam Vaughan made sure I was never on camera. He understood completely. He said, "If I was living down here, my dad wouldn't understand." We used to talk about his dad (journalist Colin Vaughan). Adam would come down without a camera and bring us things like snowmobile boots, because frostbite was a big problem.

There was one newspaper article that said panhandlers were making $200 to $300 a day! Let's face it, a lot of us at Tent City drank. We drank for the same reason people who sleep outside might drink. It makes the concrete softer. It makes whatever you're sleeping in softer or warmer, or you don't feel the cold as much. Except for Christmas, if you make $20 in a day that's not a bad day. If you make more, that's a good day. A guy in a car once threw a loonie at me and I caught it in the cup. He said, "I'm going to keep throwing 'til you miss." Another time a car pulled up at our corner. I told Nancy, "He's going to give us some money." The light was changing to green and the driver shouted, "One of you'd better get over here." I said, "Nancy, you can move faster." My knees are buggered up. So she runs out and he gives us $20. Once in a while you get a little gift like that. But panhandlers have seen a backlash, sometimes after biased stories in the media like the so-called Queen's Park Riot (the Ontario Coalition Against Poverty protest at Queen's Park in June, 2000, where a violent confrontation with police was wrongly blamed on the protestors), or the "shaky lady story"(the story about the older woman who panhandled and reportedly would be picked up by her son and taken home to her apartment every day).

The winter we had generators only two of us were home on New Year's Eve, 2000. Nancy had gone to an Out of the Cold at McCaul and Dundas to take care of her frostbitten toes. I was in the camper with the light on. Panning had been good that day. There was a knock at the door and a reporter and photographer were standing there. They were expecting to see Nancy. They said, "We know you don't talk to us, Marty, but there's no one else down here but you." "Okay," I said, "I'll answer your questions, but the first time you ask me a stupid question, the interview is over." The first question they asked was, "As we enter the new millennium, what does this mean to you as a resident of Tent City?" I said, "Well, look at that. Your first question is stupid!" And I closed the door. I'm trying to keep from freezing to death, and they ask me about the new millennium!

The *Toronto SUN*, in all the time we were there, never had one good word to say about us. Never once. I don't know where they got some of their stories, like about us eating the animals down there, the groundhogs, the ducks, the geese, the squirrels. Maybe columnist Heather Bird had a dream and decided they should write an article about it, I don't know. We were feeding, not eating, one of the groundhogs. We'd named him Gordie. They would come at first light with the ducks quacking at our door, saying "Come on – get up, we want our stale bread from all the sandwiches that were donated." The *Toronto SUN* printed two letters of rebuttal from me and Nancy. But of course they made smart-ass comments at the end of the letters. Sue-Ann Levy wrote in the *SUN*, a year after we got our housing, that she couldn't believe that 94 percent of us were still housed. She thought we'd end up choosing to go back to the street! She was man enough to say, "I have to eat my words." Earlier she'd written a really scathing article about us jumping the queue for this housing.

My best experience with a journalist was with Larry Krotz of the *National Post*. He took his time and never pressured us. Most of the interviews were over breakfast, down at a Cherry Street restaurant. Or April and I would take the dog for a walk and he'd join us. It wasn't just question and answer. We talked. The article in the *Post* was sympathetic and he didn't misquote us once. He even brought it over for us to check over. On the day we were evicted a photographer came to take a picture to accompany the article. We didn't want it taken in front of the security

> **Letter to the Editor, *Toronto SUN*, July 18, 2001**
> Re: "HOMELESS Cookin'" (July 13): As a senior resident of Tent City (18–plus months) I have never seen any abuse, let alone poaching of the wildlife here. Fruit that is past its prime is left out for the gopher and its kids. The ducks visit the campsite in the early morning and evening to be hand-fed stale bread. An appearance at the sea wall is an open invitation to scores of Canada geese for a free snack. An orphaned raccoon baby was adopted until it could fend for itself. The dogs on site are so used to these happenings it doesn't even rate their attention. I consider this article insulting.
>
> – Martin Lang, Tent City, Toronto

guards so we went down to Cherry Beach for the picture. My parents were no longer alive at this point.

The day we were evicted was the worst day of my life.

That day, April and I had left first thing in the morning. We were on our way back to Tent City and as we walked by the restaurant on Cherry Street there were about fifteen police cars there. I said to her, "Boy, they must be shooting some big movie," because they shot a lot of movies around there. We'd been up late drinking, so we went home and went to sleep. We weren't awake when the police entered Tent City. There was a knock on the door. I got up and I opened it, and there are six or seven police officers, and a bunch of security guards, and a couple of animal control officers.

"Okay," they said, "you're the last two to be evicted." I said, "We're being evicted?" I went out and walked up to one of the police officers who used to stop at Tent City and talk with us sometimes. "What's going on?" I asked. "Why are you evicting us?" And he says, "We're not evicting you. Home Depot is evicting you. That's why *their* security guards are here. We're here to make sure everything is peaceful." So I go in and wake April up, get the dog, and they say, "You have two minutes." But the police officer said, "It's gonna be a stretched two minutes. Pack what you need." So we did, more or less, in a bundle-buggy and two knapsacks. At the time we were being evicted we didn't know where we were going to go that night. April wasn't in good shape, so the female officer took her to 55 Division so she could lie down for a few hours.

I saw a lot of the media there, and I know Cathy's cell phone must have been burning, getting everyone there. Even people from the local St. Lawrence neighbourhood came by. They had always been supportive. People at the community centre had always let us use the showers and the swimming pool. The coffee shop guy would always give us a wave. We were no trouble to them.

We were a bunch of lost souls that day. Nobody in the media, not a single one, got in our faces. Larry from the *Post* came over and gave me some money. An older lady from a nearby condominium brought some money too. She said, "Well, when I saw you two walking your dog every morning, I would know you'd made it through another night."

I had to leave all my tools behind. But far more importantly, the family photos. As my mum and dad got older they divided the family photos according to who was in them, and gave them to us. I had pictures of me at home in my navy uniform, pictures of my brother's wedding when I was best man, and pictures of us at our cottage when we were kids. April and I couldn't pack things like that, and we were told they'd be safe. My father, George Lang, had been awarded the second-highest medal during the Second World War. He would never talk about it. When I got older he gave me a *Sudbury Star* article written during the war, saying that he'd been awarded this medal, but he still wouldn't talk about it. The presentation took place at a meeting in the small town in northern Ontario where he came from. A friend of mine had framed it for me. I had to leave it behind. My mum's obituary too. Pictures of my mum and dad at their fiftieth wedding anniversary. Stuff like that is priceless. I didn't recover any of it. I think our claim with Home Depot for our lost belongings is history.

They told us we had sixty or ninety days, I forget which, to get the rest of our things. A couple of days after the eviction, we got a bit more stuff because by then we were being put up in the gymnasium at Woodgreen Community Centre. Tent City looked like a concentration camp. Home Depot had put up a fifteen-foot fence with razor wire on top. Two weeks later we went back again, because April now had housing and we were going to take personal stuff to her place. An older lady from the nearby Gooderham & Worts neighbourhood came by, and she offered to go in with April and help her bring things out. I told her I didn't think the guards would let her in, and she said, "You watch me!" – she was a feisty old girl. "We think about you over there," she said. Well, we found the inside of our house had been completely trashed. They had a perimeter fence and security guards every fifteen or twenty feet to safeguard our stuff. How did that happen?

That eviction was rude. To be told that you have a few minutes to pack up stuff and then to go back and find that everything had been ransacked!

I went for a walk by there recently, and it looks like Ground Zero. They still haven't done anything with the property. I didn't think the City would let them put a 70,000 square foot big-box store down there. Developers recently went to the City and proposed eleven highrise towers, two of them more than fifty storeys tall, a big-box store and a massive parking garage. The City said no! I was ecstatic when I read that decision. It's about time they got it where they gave it to us. I think Home Depot will sell with a loss, and I hope they eat it. I read where Home Depot had another record-breaking year in profits, which means the consumers are paying for land that can't be used. It's a real waste.

There are places where you could put a tent, and they would never see it until the leaves fell off. Like where the original twelve of us were. There's no security down there anymore. I won't say how but if anyone's stuck in the spring, well, they should get set up in there as soon as the leaves are on the bushes. Now they're talking about using the land if we get the next Olympic bid – yeah, right, a pipe dream. Contaminated land! Who wants to decontaminate the land? I'm going to love walking down there this summer, as it sits empty waiting to be redeveloped, and just sort of thumb my nose at Home Depot.

There was chaos with the eviction, and then a little bit of calm began to come out of the chaos. I understand that through TDRC there was some political pressure to treat us like humans, and I know there was some political maneuvering just to get us into Woodgreen. That community centre opened its doors for us. All of a sudden we had a place to go. Some people were put up in motels right away, but had to send their pets to the Humane Society. Woodgreen had also set aside a special room for people and their pets. Almost out of nothing we had a whole social system working to get us housed. Within hours we had an infrastructure. It was amazing how fast it all happened. Every morning social services came and gave out food vouchers. Within forty-eight hours the rent supplement program was negotiated. Then, within two weeks after the eviction, we started housing people.

The Emergency Homelessness Pilot Project provided rent supplements for the people evicted from Tent City. Those monies would top up what people could pay for rent, and allow people to actually afford housing in the private sector. The program also provided housing support workers who helped people find and keep their housing. They also helped them navigate the bureaucratic red tape, like getting approved for disability, or obtaining their ID.

At first I was housed in the downtown core, which is what I wanted and waited for. They tried to organize it the way we'd tried to do with the prefab houses at Tent City. Those who had been there the longest got first choice. But I didn't want to live out by the airport or at Jane and Steeles or at the end of the Scarborough Rapid Transit Line. April took a place at Jane and Steeles, but I stayed downtown, sleeping outside at Nathan Phillips Square. I used to go on the bus out there and visit her every weekend. As I got off the bus, I'd have to walk past a sign that says "Welcome to Toronto." The first time I went to visit her, she says, "I know what you're gonna do first. You're gonna flick lights on and off and flush the toilet." And that's exactly what I did. The gym-shelter at Woodgreen finally shut, so TDRC bought a few tents for a few of us to sleep in at the park beside Jimmy Simpson rec centre.

There was pressure for us to succeed in the housing. I'm really amazed that the majority of the people have done well in the places they've been put into. Ninety percent of us are still housed. It's been a roaring success. I'm surprised, because one of the reasons we moved into Tent City was because we were a bunch of so-called "screw-ups" who didn't like society, more or less. We'd lived in rooming houses and Cockroach Lane housing projects, and we'd just had enough. So at Tent City we were our own landlord – it was a kind of freedom. To be put back into housing, into society, to deal with the bureaucracy of different social assistance programs – it really surprised me that everyone did so well with it.

I've been homeless or underhoused for seventeen of the last twenty-one years. Today – I've got my own place. But since we were evicted from Tent City, I've had to move three times. The buildings I was in were infested with bedbugs. The landlord would spray, but two days later the eggs would hatch and they'd be coming out of the baseboards and up between the tiles in the bathroom. In one year, in one apartment, I had to throw out all my belongings three times! Those bugs get into everything!

My new apartment is really great. It's air conditioned, and I face south towards the lake. It's got a huge kitchen, and the bedroom has a skylight, so it's bright and airy. It's above a flower shop and an Ethiopian coffee house. My next door neighbour is my close friend Heartbeat from Tent City. The rent is $850 a month. My disability cheque covers a portion and the rent supplement covers the remainder. The Furniture Bank provided me with a bed. Barb Craig, a nurse from Street Health, gave me a couch and a chair and a coffee maker. The Sanctuary drop-in gave me knives and forks. People don't realize when someone gets housing, they still need sheets and pillows and all the other fixings. By the end of this summer I hope to be very comfortable in East York, and get involved in the neighbourhood. I'm leaving some of my downtown roots behind.

I've also got a new doctor. Dr. Jamie Read is a homeless advocate, a real down-to-earth guy. Everyone says I'm looking well. I've got a few health problems, but I'm taking care of them. It's my fifty-year retrofit. That's what they call it in the navy when your ship is fixed up every four years to make it last another four. When I joined the navy in 1973, my ship, the *Kootenay*, was already over twenty years old. I've been to an orthopedic surgeon about my knee. He told me he had bragging rights because his wife had followed me in the media from day one during the news coverage of the Tent City eviction. My knee replacement should be done before Christmas.

I've even had a liver biopsy. I've decided to take the Interferon and hope it will eradicate the Hepatitis C from my liver. I just got new reading glasses and my teeth are next. By 2007 I'll be good for another fifty years.

I keep busy. I volunteer with the TDRC, with the Ryerson food bank, the Church of the Holy Trinity's breakfast program, and with the Sanctuary. I was the president of the High C group at my church when I was growing up. We helped the community. It's like being a cub or a scout. I've been helping people in the community since I was five years old!

Growing up, we attended church because my dad felt it was a duty. Today, religion is very important in my life. I was recently baptized at the Sanctuary. I spent most of the night before the baptism going over some hard memories.

I did a lot of soul searching. I feel like I have a lot of experiences and stories to tell, and I've started to write them down. It's helping me to come to terms with some of my memories.

I reconnected with my older sister, Georgina, at Thanksgiving. Most of my reconnection with family has been in the last year – with my sister, my younger brother, John, and my older brother, Rick.

Georgina's a retired nurse from the Calgary General. I wrote her the night before the baptism and said, "Georgina, I wish that God had an area code because I'd like to phone Mom tonight." Georgina and I talk on the phone a lot now, and we have some really good conversations. She calls me "Martin." We've got twenty years to make up for in lost time.

She didn't understand why I joined the navy. We were living in Sarnia at the time – my dad was burying the cable in southwestern Ontario. I was about sixteen and was looking after my younger brother, John, who was twelve, because my parents went to Hamilton to play bridge. My sister had two kids by then, so she had a built-in babysitter – me. I was getting dressed for a school band concert – white bell-bottoms, white turtleneck – when I heard the kids yell, "John's on fire!" He had been playing with gas on a log and the gas had spilled down his pants and into his high-top running shoes. Somehow a match was thrown on him. And I was supposed to be looking after him. So I had to phone mom and dad in Hamilton. Even though my mom understood, I always felt my dad blamed me for not looking after John properly. My brother was burnt right to the bone. He had three years of skin grafts.

So I left home. I joined the navy because of guilt. I finished high school. I didn't know what I wanted to do with my life. So I decided to see the world. My dad had been in the army. My uncle had been in the navy. I come from a long military history. All of my uncles and one of my aunts were in the military.

When I left the navy I moved to Ontario and was in touch with John, but not my mom and dad. I wasn't ready to face them. I also thought they might be disappointed I had left the navy. But, I thought to myself, I was closer in case one of them got sick, like when my dad lost his legs. I visited them then in Sault Ste. Marie, when they moved off the farm because he was in a wheelchair.

I still miss parts of Tent City – everyone gathering around the first fire of the day. Whoever got up first put water on for coffee. I miss the people who would come down to help us out. I miss all the kids' groups who used to come down because usually they would be directed to me for a talk and a tour and some history of the place. I miss all the dogs and the animals. My plan for the spring is to get a medium-sized dog. Maybe a Labrador.

The core group at Tent City (at first we called ourselves the Dirty Dozen when we were still in tents), there is still a grapevine amongst us. We still pretty well all keep in touch, enough to make sure everyone is well, and that we know what's going on in each other's lives.

I don't know why, maybe because we were in the media a lot, but as soon as you mention Tent City, it seems to open doors. The number of people you reach expands. Now people ask me for my opinion, and I never thought people would ask me for my opinion. I've decided I'm going to get more involved with groups fighting homelessness.

Now, I spend a lot of time talking to different groups. I was invited to a same-sex marriage, just from meeting people when I spoke at the Church of the Holy Trinity. I recently went to a Board meeting at the Atkinson Foundation for TDRC, up on the executive floor, with original copies of the first issues of the *Toronto Star* on the wall. I was sitting there with Cathy at a thirty-foot-long boardroom table, all polished and glistening. When one of the Board members came up and said, "Hi Marty, I haven't seen you for a long time," Crowe was surprised and gave me the "Crowe look" (she opens her eyes real wide).

Recently I did a talk to Grade 7s and showed them a video clip of our eviction. It was the first time I had seen the tape. When I looked up, some of the girls were crying. It's still hard to talk about.

I'm jotting down notes now for a national conference that I'm speaking at, and I'm hoping that the conference will open up other speaking opportunities for me. I'd be willing to travel. It's real easy to speak about Tent City. I have no problem with that. It gets easier every time. I think any type of public speaking gets easier with familiarity. I also do public speaking for the Sanctuary at some of the churches that support us. The Sanctuary gets asked to bring in someone

Marty and his friend April at Cherry Beach, after the eviction, 2002

who uses their services, and it's usually me. I don't mind speaking at City Hall, but sometimes when you speak there you feel like it's falling on deaf ears. We don't have the councillors like we used to.

I've been working with the media since we were evicted in 2002. It's important that people know about the homeless. I wanted to be more involved before that, but I couldn't while my parents were still alive. Now I can. Also I really didn't feel it was proper when we were at Tent City. I thought it was okay to talk to the media, but not to be part of an organized group, because we were still squatters and there's no such thing as squatters' rights in Canada. We had no legal right to squat. We had the right to speak, but also the right to be misquoted.

I take my work with the media pretty seriously. Even though most of us aren't homeless anymore, it's still important that people know about homelessness. Homelessness hasn't been getting much ink lately. Sometimes it seems

Marty at the Canadian Conference on Homelessness, York University, 2005

like there's something every day in the media. But lately it just seems forgotten, because people aren't sleeping at City Hall any more. There are still people on the grates. Then there was the woman who was run over by a cop car when it ran up on the sidewalk. She was five months pregnant! One mention in the paper and nothing after! It's not like she was sleeping on the road. She was sleeping on the sidewalk.

When I first moved here in 1981 I stayed in shelters like Fred Victor, when it was still a men's hostel. It was easy to get a bed in those days. I don't think they ever turned anyone away. You just walked in and they'd say, "Come back at 4 P.M. and we'll have your card." Today, even in winter, people are turned away by the hostels, which is why the Out of the Cold programs started.

Some people find they can't handle being on a mat in a church basement, three inches away from the next person. So they say, "No, I'm gonna sleep outside instead of in here." And you have people in there with mental health problems who talk to themselves all night. It makes it hard to get a night's sleep, especially when you've been tramping the streets all day.

I've been to so many memorials. I wanted to read a poem last week at the homeless memorial. It was called "Lament to a Lost Native Child." I had it in my back pocket. Nance said she would go up there with me to the microphone. I figured I was going to cry halfway through – I couldn't do it. It brought back too many memories. Recently, Remembrance Day did the same thing. When I was in the navy, my destroyer, the *Kootenay*, escorted the last Red Cross ship that was bringing the Vietnamese orphans to Canada. It was a very emotional time for everybody. Some of the kids were really sick, and they were brought over to our ship because we had the doctors. I'm reading a book now about the last days of Vietnam.

To the politicians who think they can force people to sleep in a shelter, I would say: "Have you ever walked around at 11 P.M. at night and talked to the people who are out there in their sleeping bags and asked them why they aren't inside? Well, it's because of tuberculosis, and other new epidemics, like bedbugs. And Out of the Cold spaces are for one night only. They might have eighty people for the evening and there are no shower facilities. People coming in, just lying down in their clothes."

The success of the Tent City program was partly because the first housing support workers who were hired in the program to work with us were well aware of Tent City, and they were friends to us before they became housing workers. So unless outreach and housing workers can take an interest in people, they'll get them placed, sure, but will they do the follow-up? I was voted by the tenants to sit on a City committee – I'm the CROTCH, the Client Representative of the Tent City Housing, to try to make the program work. I bring things forward that need to be addressed and try to solve them. I feel respected.

I think in five years homelessness will still be a problem. We're fighting a battle. We've got a lot of people bailing the boat but a lot of people are throwing water in it too. Sometimes it doesn't seem uphill, it seems downhill, especially when we get a kick in the ass, like an article from the *Toronto SUN*.

The only way to end this massive problem of homelessness is to push for affordable housing.

I really liked Dalton McGuinty when he got elected premier, but I haven't seen him go forward with what he promised for housing, which was twenty thousand new units.

I'd like to take the federal minister of housing out for a tour to show him or her where so many people are sleeping because they're homeless. Toronto is the worst in all of Canada. I'd take him through the hostels and show him the conditions. I do outreach with the Sanctuary, and I know all the hidden outside sleeping places. I would like to talk to him one-on-one and show him these places. I'd say to him, "Did you see some people under just a little grey Salvation Army blanket? It will be cold tonight, it might snow. I'll tell you what, I'll get two blankets, if you want to sleep out tonight." On day two of the tour when we woke up, I'd take him to the City Hall washrooms when they open. Then maybe show him 2 Murray Street – an example of the type of housing he should be building.

Where would I like to be in five years? I'd like to be the head of the TDRC. I've got the experience.

CHAPTER 6

BRIAN BOYD

THE BOY NEXT DOOR

Brian with his friend Karen and dog Chaos, 2000

Friday, December 20, 2002. Friday, the day horrible things always seem to happen. Gaetan Heroux made the call to us at the Toronto Disaster Relief Committee. I leaned heavily into the wall in the office. I cried, "No, no, Brian?" Beric's face was grim and he fell silent. This was to be one of our most bitter losses.

Here is Brian's story, partly in my words, partly in his.

– Cathy

BRIAN GREW UP IN A SMALL NORTHWESTERN ONTARIO TOWN called Atikokan, 2½ hours west of Thunder Bay. Childhood friends of Brian describe him as "the boy next door." He was smart in high school. He was a great downhill skier as a child. He loved all things electronic – CB radios, music, video. He and his friends did a DJ music show Saturdays on the local station, where they played all the popular music. He had a lot of friends and when he graduated from high school in 1982, everyone said he was going to become a big time DJ or go into broadcasting.

Brian lived in Toronto for a time, where he had his own business and a nice house. He decided to move out to British Columbia because he'd gotten fed up with the big city. He sold everything and opened a business in BC. Several years later he moved back to Toronto and found the situation completely changed. In his electronics trade the pay rates were horrible. He found himself unable to afford a place to rent and basically, as he says, "got stuck in the system."

On a bitterly cold day in 1999, five days before Christmas, the Toronto Disaster Relief Committee delivered massive "winter relief" to Tent City, a squatters' camp that had sprung up on Toronto's waterfront, nestled south of the Lakeshore near Cherry Street and the Turning Channel used by the big ships. The chunk of contaminated land had been neglected and had sat waiting. Its owner, Home Depot, was waiting to build a big-box store; Toronto's Olympic Bid

Committee was waiting to use the land for the Olympic Village, should their bid succeed; and more progressive urban leaders were waiting and hoping to wrench some green space from the corporate vultures eyeing Toronto's waterfront.

Homeless people weren't waiting any longer though, and had dug in their heels, creating a squatters' camp called Tent City. TDRC wasn't waiting any longer either, and under the masterful direction of Beric German had developed an exceptional and daring plan – to bring disaster relief into Tent City, just as if it were a natural disaster. The purpose: to stabilize Tent City, which had been recently threatened with eviction.

The relief effort had galvanized agencies, members of the faith community, and unions like the Canadian Auto Workers and the Canadian Union of Public Employees. On a bitterly cold but brilliantly sunny day, the relief was brought in. Sustenance – a full turkey dinner with stuffing and gravy, potatoes, vegetables, fruit, and cakes. Infrastructure – the delivery of a little prefab house, called a DuraKit, bought for $1 from the manufacturer by the TDRC and delivered on a flatbed truck donated by a Rotary Club member and a construction company. This was to be a test. The small prefab housing units were made in Canada, for disaster relief shelter in other parts of the world that faced natural disasters. Would they work here? We thought so. And so did Brian Boyd, who moved into one that very day.

The mood was festive. Kathy Hardill, a well known street nurse served turkey dinners wearing reindeer antlers. Other volunteers decorated small trees with Christmas decorations. Singer/activist Arlene Mantle performed. Ontario New Democratic Party leader Howard Hampton gave a speech. Federal NDP leader Jack Layton, then a city councillor and long-time champion of Tent City, spoke to the media and joined in the festivities.

But Brian Boyd, perhaps living up to his earlier interests in broadcasting, was the major spokesperson that day, and he was enthusiastic: "It's been going just great at Tent City today!!" Not missing a chance to fully explain why people were forced to create a Tent City, he continued: "The people who are on welfare and who can't work, they get $520 a month, and if you can find an apartment for $520 a month in Toronto, it's a miracle. They do have subsidized housing in

Brian with Jack Layton, on the day TDRC brought disaster relief into Tent City, 2000

Toronto, but the waiting list is seven to eight years at least, if you qualify to get in. So as far as affordable housing goes, in Toronto it's non-existent. This could be a prototype. People can see how it's going to work out on a smaller basis, and then maybe they could start looking at other sites to put up more."

Up until that day Brian had been living on the Home Depot land with his girlfriend, Karen, and Chaos, their aptly named dog, in a makeshift shelter with a blue tarp protecting them from the wind and snow. They had sleeping bags, a couch dropped off by a film crew, a candle, and a radio.

Brian described that early period to filmmaker Michael Connolly:

> We built ourselves a little shelter and it kind of caught the attention of
> the media and then the media attention really hit full force with the
> help of the Toronto Disaster Relief Committee. They arranged to have
> these houses and the generator and a few other things. And because

of the media we had a lot of people bringing down clothes and food. There were a lot of people living down here for some time who just basically didn't like the idea of a hostel.

Brian went on to explain the difficulties of hostel living:

> First off, the hostels don't take couples, okay, and Karen and I have a dog and so there is absolutely no place that would allow you to go with a dog. A lot of these places we had to go last year, they're called Out of the Cold – places that just open up in the wintertime, and they're scattered all over the city so you have to go to a different location every night, which means that everything you bring with you, you have to take with you during the day and bring it to the next place you go. So you can't really accumulate possessions because you have no place to put them. You go into this one particular overnight hostel, it's like the last straw, the last place you can go. You go in at 8 P.M. when it opens and find a space on the floor and they give you a thin exercise mat. There's no bedding. You wake up at 1 A.M. and everyone has come in off the street and you can't even move.

Brian and Karen were chosen to be the new residents of the first DuraKit brought into Tent City.

The opening narration from "Shelter from the Storm," the documentary by Michael Connolly, describes the scene:

> This open lot on the windy shore of Lake Ontario is probably the coldest spot in the whole city. Residents face frostbite through the winter. A few weeks before Christmas a volunteer organization known as the Toronto Disaster Relief Committee brought in a factory-made shelter called a DuraKit, and a Tent City couple moved in. The tiny prefab house is actually meant for disaster relief for the victims of flood and war. The TDRC sees homelessness as a national disaster.

During this narration Karen is shown sweeping the porch on the little house and Brian is out front chopping wood. They are modern images of pioneers on Toronto's waterfront. A banner saying "Disaster House" hangs on the DuraKit. These images were all over the news, national, and local for weeks.

Brian, Karen, and Chaos spent that first night in a brand new, clean place of their own – the tiny, 8×12 foot, fibreboard DuraKit. The unit would normally sell for $2,500, and has a lifespan of 50 to 100 years. DuraKits are used all around the world for rehousing people temporarily. Ironically, Canada is one of the few countries not to use them, even though they are made here.

Brian was always to the point in his media interviews, clear about his role, and the reasons for setting up a squatter camp:

> It's impossible to find affordable housing in Toronto. It's a really, really desperate situation, which is why there are so many people living on the streets and in hostel situations. Karen and I used to come down here with a couple friends of ours, oh, this is going back a couple of years. We used to come down here just to get away from the mainstream and have a few beers and relax, in a place where the police wouldn't harass us. I'm not too worried about the contamination and in my honest opinion contaminated land is everywhere on the waterfront.
>
> Eventually Karen and I were staying at a place that was an overnight hostel, very overcrowded, and then they announced they were going to close the place down. The chances for us to be together in a shelter are almost non-existent, plus we have a dog – it just totally eliminates the possibility. So Karen and I thought about coming down here, and there were already a couple of people set up with tents. So Karen and I originally set up a tent. The people who had been living here for some time basically didn't like the idea of the hostel system. We wanted to be separated a bit from the mainstream.
>
> We've been working with the media to try to bring attention to a serious problem here in Toronto and all across Canada. We're trying

to show that there's an alternative solution to just opening up more hostels.

I love all the media attention because we're trying to make a statement about homelessness in Toronto, homelessness all across Canada. So this is what we wanted to do, and this is what's happening, so it just makes me happy.

I'd like to see the government subsidize affordable housing for people.

Media documented every aspect of Tent City life. In an interview regarding the generators, Brian said, "It's a really efficient unit, and it hasn't burned a drop of oil. Pat and I fill it up every day and take care of it to make sure it's running properly." The public liked Brian's pioneering nature.

Brian was quite engaged in planning, and working towards a long-term solution for Tent City. He had the foresight and positive attitude to know that the momentum behind Tent City meant that the prefab concept could evolve into a solution to the shelter crisis. At a city hall meeting where Tent City members and TDRC were planning the relocation of Tent City, he remarked: "This could be a prototype as well. They [the City] could see how this would work out on a smaller basis and maybe they could look at other sites and try it somewhere else."

If only the City could be so committed.

Brian was insistent that Tent City was a stepping stone that provided freedom and dignity for himself and others. In another media interview he described their efforts:

What we're trying to do here, as well as help ourselves, which is what we've basically done 'til now, is to work with the media to bring attention to the fact that there is a real serious problem here and all across Canada. It's very hard work now, it's very hard. This is a temporary home base. If we find a new place to put these things (prefab houses), or if we set this place up more as a permanent location, then it's very workable. It's pretty hard to go into a job interview carrying a sleeping bag and a knapsack.

If we're moved on to City-owned property... and like we discussed at the meeting, the management of services is taken care of – for example making sure the water is okay, the showers are clean, the toilets are clean, the garbage, I don't think people will mind that. But people don't want to be managed, we want to be self-governed.

Down here, the people that live down here get along pretty well. We all know each other, and we all know we don't have to worry about each other. In fact, we can count on someone if we need help. That's one thing we're really trying to stress here. We think we can make this a prototype and make it work, and we're working really hard and we've been putting a lot of effort into it so far. If we can prove it's a workable, feasible system, then we hope we can expand it for people.

At a press conference held in front of Toronto City Hall, regarding a second threatened eviction (ironically the City's 2008 Olympic bid banner hung as a backdrop), Brian matter-of-factly described the benefits of Tent City as a community: "We can go down there and come and go as we please. So to me, and to a lot of people down there, it's one step before getting into real housing."

Brian was especially articulate about the housing crisis:

Right now, the last I heard, the vacancy rate is 2 or 3 percent, which means it's practically impossible to find a place, and if you can find a place it's going to cost you a lot of money. So people that are, say, on disability or welfare or even CPP, or whatever, it's impossible for them to find affordable housing in Toronto and it's a really, really desperate situation, which is why there are so many people living on the streets and in hostel situations.

You can't survive on $6 or $7 an hour. Even at $10 an hour you're scraping by. The last job I had in Toronto they were paying $10 an hour, and I'm a very well qualified person – my specialty is two-way radio communications and TV/VCR repairs. For me to go to work for $10 an hour as an electronics technician, for someone who is charging $60 or $70 an hour for my labour…this is totally ridiculous for someone with my education and experience in the field.

On the Monday morning, September 11, 2001, I was just learning of the twin towers when Beric phoned to tell me that we had had a fire at Tent City. The DuraKit had burned. At that time Brian was living in the DuraKit with his best friend, the Colonel. Brian and the Colonel were now made homeless – literally. The Colonel, badly burned, had been admitted to St. Michael's Hospital. Brian was traumatized.

This was a major setback for Brian.

After the fire, Brian spent a lot of time at the Seaton House Annex, and subsequently at numerous Out of the Colds, forced to move nightly due to the nature of the volunteer program. This constant movement from one church basement to another clearly wore him down. He visited the Colonel daily in St. Michael's hospital. They were inseparable. After the Tent City eviction, Beric worked to see if Brian and the Colonel would be eligible for the Tent City housing program. They were.

Brian continued to speak out, especially during a particularly harsh police crackdown on people living outdoors.

He had received eight tickets from the police in one night, while sitting in a park where he was waiting for a shelter to open.

Brian spoke with then CBC news reporter Tracy Moore: "The eight tickets I have here are from just one night – 'loitering in a public place.' The officer that gave me the ticket said, 'Look, I know you guys aren't going to pay this ticket.' I guess they have to make their quota." Although Brian was speaking to the media about the tickets, he made sure the reporters made the connection to the bigger issue of homelessness, by reminding them he was stuck living out on the street because there was no affordable housing.

The week before Brian died, the Colonel and Brian had panhandled for enough money to rent a room in order to have a break from the Out of the

Cold program. When the Colonel tried to rouse Brian in the morning, he didn't wake up.

The gap left by Brian's death was palpable everywhere. It still is, really.

Greg Paul from the Sanctuary, a drop-in, described Brian as a "long-time friend who helped us to serve meals to other people, and he was obviously very involved in advocacy as well."

The Colonel: "It just feels like there's a part of me missing, like someone tore my soul out or something."

Those who knew him said he was political, an activist, and a good friend.

In media coverage after Brian's death there were reminders of how in his last days Brian's choices for shelter were crowded church basements, or outdoor spaces where he was persecuted – repeatedly visited and ticketed by police. As Beric German remarked, "This is the same process occurring across Canada and the United States. It's sometimes referred to as 'Mean Sweeps' or the 'New York Model.' Maybe Brian was ill, but why should he have been treated like that, to wander, to be pushed like that from one crowded place to the other?"

A memorial for Brian's life was held in All Saints Church on January 10th, 2003. All Saints was packed. Brian's mom and dad came from Atikokan.

Today, a picture of Brian looks down over the very card table in All Saints where the Colonel and many others still sit, reading the paper, staying warm, waiting for housing. The room is always full.

CHAPTER 7

THE COLONEL

TOWN CRIER

The Colonel remembering Brian, New Year's Day, 2003

You can tell from his name that he's probably a bit of a legend, and more than a little bit of fun. You know, like in the old game of Clue: "the Colonel in the conservatory with the candlestick." He's had a life of mischief, to say the least.

But the Colonel is clearly liked, respected, and trusted on the street. He's got a heart of gold and would give you the coat off his back if you needed it. His voice is like sandpaper, and when the Colonel speaks, you listen. He's a natural leader. And… he's a great hugger.

I've been touched by how he channels his sadness over the state of homelessness into passionate speech and action.

The Colonel and I spent some time in Allan Gardens, which was once his home. He reflected on the time he was homeless, and the role he has played speaking out. While we sat on the bench, people were constantly walking by, nodding to him, or saying, "Hi Colonel," showing him respect. He is a street celebrity. He is known. On other days we met in All Saints Church in a cubicle that staff let us use – kind of like his private office.

– Cathy

I WAS BORN IN 1949 IN MISCOUCHE, PRINCE EDWARD ISLAND. MY mom had fourteen children. There were three sets of twins that died at birth or shortly afterwards, and there were eight surviving kids.

My early years were tough. My dad was a carpenter by trade but unfortunately he was an alcoholic. He would get his cheque and not give any money to my mom, so she had to go out and work just to keep us in food. I remember being around eight years old and seeing him beat her. She eventually kicked him out and we got rid of him. Back in those days, before my mom and dad broke up, one parent could sign the papers to put their kids in an orphanage. Well, he did that. He figured he would have more money, I guess. My mom later met Aubrey, who became my step-dad. One day, when I was around twelve, my brother Gary and I were altar boys, and my mom arrived on Sunday to say "you're coming home." We threw off our altar gowns and we ran. We were so happy. Aubrey worked for the town of Summerside as a diesel engineer, running all the electrical. He fed us and supported us. He lived a very good life, but unfortunately he died from Alzheimers.

My real dad is dead now.

I finished high school with Grade 12 general and then went back to get my "academic" Grade 12 diploma. Then, I went to the University of Prince Edward Island, but only for a month. I joined the military when I was twenty-two. I spent four years in Air Traffic Control.

I could do drywall, floors, tile, everything under the sun, and I took a tile setting course at Holland College where they train you to tile walls, cars, floors, anything. There wasn't much of a future in PEI for anyone with my qualifications, because they weren't paying much money. So I said to myself, I spent ten years in Air Cadets and I know all the drill and all the basic training, so I might as well join the military. So I went to Halifax and I wrote tests for two days. Then they came back with the results and they said, "Well what do you want to be?" I said, "Well, what can you offer me, what am I qualified for?" They said, "With your qualifications – you've got grade 12 education, one month of university – we'll start you at Camp Borden."

Then for Air Traffic Control training I went down to Cornwallis in Nova Scotia.

That's a boot camp where you go through your military training, your physical and shooting. Then I was a qualified air traffic controller, B stand. I got my papers and they moved me to Chatham, New Brunswick. I told them that I had lived in the Maritimes most of my life and I wanted to go to Vancouver, I wanted to see Canada. They told me that after they sent me to Chatham they'd give me preference posting and I'd go to Vancouver. Next time my posting came up it was Greenwood, Nova Scotia. I said "you're going the wrong direction guys," and then after Greenwood they transferred me to Summerside, PEI, for two years! After Summerside they posted me in Goose Bay, Labrador, so I spent a year and a half there. Then my four years were up and they wanted to promote me to Corporal and ship me over to Baden-Baden in Germany to complete my training with a radar course, and to keep me in the military. I told them they're nuts. I said I can't stand your little rules and regulations.

I left PEI for the first time in 1970, and I still miss it. I eventually moved to Ottawa to be near my sister, and then in 1989 I moved to Toronto. I still go home to Summerside to visit my mom who's still alive – she's eighty-two. She has cataracts in one eye and her legs are starting to get feeble. She worked hard all her life, on her hands and knees, scrubbing the floors of doctors and lawyers. My sisters Geraldine and Alma live close to her and take care of her.

Most of my time in Toronto, I've been homeless. I met a really good friend named Brian at Satan House [*sic*] when I first came to Toronto. Brian was like my street brother. We started to go to the Out of the Cold programs when they first started up, but sometimes they'd be full, just like they are now. So we'd just take sleeping bags and we'd sleep outside. Brian and I both loved the outdoors. Snow didn't bother us. We'd double up the sleeping bags and we'd both crawl in. Then we'd throw two more sleeping bags over the top of us and we'd always be warm, and we'd sit there and we'd talk about our lives and what had happened, and Brian would tell me about when he was young. He was a disc jockey and he once went down to the States and his father didn't know he left and all of a sudden one day he turns on the radio and he hears Brian's voice! So his dad went down to the States and brought him back home!

Brian and I stayed in shelters too. We lived at Street City for a while, and then after it closed Brian moved to Tent City, and then when he broke up with Karen he said, "Come and live with me." So he gave me the bed because I have a bad back, and he slept on the floor, and we were having the life of Riley. We went over to the Humane Society and got Chaos, our dog, our mascot. He's a very large King Shepherd. He's very, very large. He weighs about a hundred and thirty pounds now. He drags me around.

Before I moved into Tent City I had been homeless about fifteen years, mostly living outside. Tent City was *freedom* for us. We didn't have a curfew to be in at a certain time.

Brian and the Colonel – together

There are two people that can best judge and describe the influential effect that Brian Boyd and the Colonel have had in the housing movement. Beric German and Gaetan Heroux have each worked at "the corner" [Sherbourne and Dundas] longer than anyone else I know. In fact, Beric and Gaetan almost mirror the qualities of the friendship they witnessed between Brian and the Colonel.

– Cathy

Gaetan: It's almost impossible to talk about the Colonel without talking about Brian. It's hard to separate the two. I associate the Colonel with Brian.

Beric: I think what I recall about these guys, both of them, is that people loved them. They were very generous with their friends, so people would always know about them. They would leave a trail, sometimes good feelings, and sometimes not, but you'd always know that they'd been there. And always when there were actions, any time when there was a protest, they were there. They also played the role of alerting people in the community – "there is an action, this is the action," and they didn't just do it verbally, they handed out flyers, they would cross the city, they would go into different drop-ins, week-ends and otherwise. They would ask to do that. Simply put, they always spoke out. So the Colonel, who is with us, still does that.

Gaetan: I first knew them from my work at Central Neighbourhood House. Both of them had a really hard time at Seaton House. For reasons that were really quite trivial, they were barred from there. If one didn't get into a shelter, in general the

Brian and I were both trained paramedics so when we were homeless we walked around the streets and if someone had a cut we'd decorate him up with a bandage. Street nurses gave us our supplies. We would go around and tell people it was dangerous to sleep on the grates because the steam rises up and other wouldn't go in. If Brian couldn't get in – the Colonel would stay out with him. Their friends would bring food and blankets out to them. I think they got barred largely because they were outspoken – and would talk about it if they didn't like something. If something happened they would say , "I don't like what I saw." So I remember them having a hard, hard time with that whole bureaucracy. And it's interesting, for all the years I knew them, the ten years I worked at Central Neighbourhood House, I never had to bar them.

Beric: They just stood up. They were the street critics. They had both lived a pretty tough life. But they didn't just accept everything that happened to them. They stood up and said something about it and then people would know about it. They were important to us in our movement. They were an alert to us as to what was going down. Was somebody being abused by the police? Were people getting ticketed? Were people getting targeted? What were the services like? What were the shelters like? Some people who would use those services would be a little frightened, they would be afraid of being barred or banned if they were to say something against them. That didn't matter for the Brian and the Colonel. They spoke out all the time. They gave evidence on the shelters on a consistent basis so that we could take that evidence and change some of the conditions. They helped to open shelters because they were there and participated when we protested. They knew the issues and then they'd end up living in the shelter they opened. So, they'd test them out.

Gaetan: And then any day you could come into the Open Door drop-in in the church and they'd be sitting there, at the same table, reading newspapers, religiously, every day. Brian's picture is up in that church, right there where he used to sit.

causes your body to sweat, and then you can freeze to death. Or we'd tell people where to get sleeping bags or blankets, and where to sleep where it's dry, like places that have an overhang. I have my medical kit with me right now. Just the other day I helped decorate a guy's wound. Hydrogen peroxide, disinfect

Beric: Brian has a contingent of admirers and that's why his photo is still on the wall. Brian and the Colonel were good friends to others. They had a friend – Silent Sam [Sam Ash]. They would always be around him. Sam couldn't speak or talk. They were his friend, to this person who lived in a world of silence. They spoke with him.

Gaetan: I have an image of the "crew" outside the church, and the hands just flying in the air.

Beric: They took the time to be with a man who is hard to communicate with, and certainly could have been very, very lonely, and they encouraged all of his efforts and the notion that he was Sam Ash the artist! They did what they could to help Sam's career and they introduced him to Danielle, who then also supported him. They were with him as friends when there was a resurgence of Sam's career. Here were these guys who had been with him and thought he was a great artist, and then they are with him when he becomes famous again for his painting.

Gaetan: Oh… to step into that room when Sam had his first gallery show in Windsor and to see seventy or eighty paintings….

Gaetan: So now the Colonel is without Brian. I can still remember the image – the Colonel just had to be out there, at the corner, outside. He would have to tell the story, how Brian died – "this is how it happened – this is how he died." The whole grieving process on the street – because there's nowhere to do that. That's a scene we see all the time.

Beric: And yet, I think the one thing about these guys was that even though they were living such a tough life, there was a lot of joy, a sense of humour, and people enjoyed being near them.

it all, wrap the wound. I told him it's too late to get sutures, but go see your doctor for the special surgical tape they can use to seal the wound. I got that training in the army. Brian was a trained paramedic in BC.

Brian and I got involved in housing and political stuff around the same time, through OCAP (the Ontario Coalition Against Poverty) and the TDRC.

We started going to all the different rallies and protests. I call them protests and rallies because that's exactly what they are, and they're peaceful. They're rallies for the homeless people, so we go to them and speak out. And because we were both educated – actually Brian also went to university – the organizers would always ask us to speak about homelessness because they knew that we had a brain and we weren't simple-minded, or anything like that, and we would tell the truth because it was the truth.

We would talk about how the government treats homeless people, how they never really help them out or care about them, how it costs over $20,000 a year to keep a person in a homeless shelter, and how that money could be used instead to put that person into housing. I talk about how the governments refuse to create subsidized housing, and how they put people on a waiting list for ten years, and by that time half of them die because of exposure to the extreme elements and stuff. We would say, look we know that some people are starting to get housing, okay, but it's not fast enough because people are still dying on the street, and there needs to be a real housing program set up.

We spoke at rallies in Ottawa, Toronto, Quebec City. In Hamilton we had the Steelworkers Union with us, and we spoke about the homeless in Toronto and Hamilton and Ottawa and all over Canada, reminding them that it's not just a Toronto problem, and the Canadian government is doing nothing about it. When TDRC brought Alexa McDonaugh, who was the federal NDP leader, on a tour of Toronto's disaster, I spoke at that meeting.

I went to Mayor Mel Lastman's New Year's Day Levee at Toronto City Hall. Cathy stayed right beside me. He comes out and he's dangling keys, key chains, giving one to everyone that comes through the lineup. He says, "Here's a key chain for you." I go, "What good is a key chain when I don't even have a door or a house to put it in?" I told him, "YOU are responsible for this, YOU are supposed to give us affordable housing." I held a picture of Brian up and showed it to him. I said "See, my friend died because you wouldn't give him housing, and how many more people have been lost? I don't even have that many fingers to count them. Frank died, Hoyte died, Brian died, Jesse died." I kept rhyming off these different names and afterwards the camera crews caught me off to the side and I gave them an interview. I basically told them what was going on and explained everything – like how we need affordable housing because someone could apply for welfare and get $525, but if their rent is $500 what are they supposed to eat? I added that they still can't afford a phone or TV or anything like that. So then, that's why people have to go and try to find a spot where other people are living outside, like we did at Tent City.

On September 11, exactly the same day and year the planes crashed into the towers in New York, we had a fire at Tent City. About four in the morning I woke up and I could smell smoke and there were flames about six feet high from the floor of our DuraKit house. I hit Brian and yelled, "Quick, we gotta get out, we're on fire, someone set fire to us!" All I had on was a pair of sport shorts, and as soon as I swung my feet over to the floor my feet stuck right to it. The heat had melted the paint. Then, soon as Brian opened the door, the flames shot up three feet high. Now I gotta walk across this floor and then when I walked through the fire I got burned, especially on the right leg, and I just dove out the door and Brian caught me. We went across the road and then we're sitting there, in shock. Why would someone set fire to us? The fire trucks and the ambulance came and they put out the fire, and they took one look at me and they took me to the hospital.

All you could see was bone and something like a gel on my left leg. They took me to St. Michael's Hospital and I had surgery – skin grafts. I was there for eight weeks. Brian came every day. Our friend Randy took Chaos for us.

After that, Art Manuel from the Seaton House Annex came to see me and said I could recuperate there, to make sure the skin grafts really took. I said, well, I can't move there unless Brian is allowed to come with me, we're street brothers and we've been street brothers for years. Because, where was Brian going to go? He was made homeless by that fire. Well, Brian got a bed there too and we were in the same room with Silent Sam. We had known him for years and we had formed our own sign language to talk to him.

Even though we had been living at Tent City we always kept up on the news. So especially after the 9/11 affair in the States, even though our fire was the same day, everyone at Tent City was still worried about what was happening in the world.

Just before Brian died we were getting so many tickets from the police for drinking in the parks. If there's a guy in a park with a three-piece suit and a bottle of wine, drinking his wine, reading his newspaper, they wouldn't bug him, but if you're a homeless person drinking in the park, you get a ticket and nine times out of ten they'll pour your beer out. I got ten tickets in two days once. Each one for $130. I said to the police, "What are you wasting your time for? We can't pay it." So we give our tickets to OCAP, and they have lawyers who fight the tickets for us. Some are young student lawyers, and they're getting the experience and also learning how to stick up for homeless people. Like the nurses and doctors fighting for people to get the Special Diet allowance – so that people can eat. At least when the police are on their work-to-rule action, they leave us alone.

Homeless people are not treated as first-class, not even second-class citizens. If you sleep on a park bench, they kick you out. "Sorry, we got zero tolerance." I say poor people pay taxes too.

I'm in the Tent City housing program now. I pay a portion of the rent and the program covers the remainder. I love it, it's beautiful. When I first walked into the bedroom of my first apartment all I had was a sleeping bag. I slept on the floor and I'm looking around this great big bedroom. I thought I had died and gone to heaven. Having my own place now, a one bedroom, with my own bed, my own place with my own furniture and everything – it's great.

I've had to move a few times though, because of the bed bug situation in these places. Toby and Vicki from Street Survivors helped me get furniture from the Furniture Bank, and my bed from Sleep Country.

I've got a place! I don't have to worry about whether it's going to snow, whether it's going to rain. I can just walk over, turn the key. I have my own place to lock the door. No one comes in unless I want them to. I feel secure. I don't have to worry about being beaten, like Paul Croutch, the man who was beaten to death in his sleeping bag in Moss Park. That makes me feel sad when

The Colonel speaking at a press conference, Sherbourne and Dundas, 2006

I think that someone can actually do physical harm to homeless people because they're homeless. Life is too valuable. I cannot believe I lived to be fifty-six years of age and I never had any problems. I slept in Allan Gardens, a big chunk of my life, slept in sleeping bags there with Brian, but we never had any problems.

I'm on ODSP (Ontario Disability Support Program) because I've got degenerative disc disease in my spine, arthritis from my toes to my hair, a shoulder that pops out on me all the time. My doctor took one look at my x-rays and CT scans and said if I was a building he'd condemn me. The doctor doesn't want to operate yet because the fusion would give me less movement. I was a member of the Maritime Tile Setters Union – I could tile vans, cars, and this church. I could be making $30 to $40 an hour. It's very specialized work.

My health has improved dramatically since I got housing. I'm drinking a smoother beer now. I can drink a few and still stay active in my brain. I have a regular routine. I leave home at six every morning to come down to the drop-in to see my friends. Every night I go home and make a pot of soup, stew really, it goes on the stove. I go to the food bank at the church. My favourite meal, if I could afford it, would be lobster.

Yesterday I spoke at a rally at the church, about the murder of this homeless man. Like I said, I don't need a microphone. You want me to talk about being homeless, I'll tell you about homelessness. I've lived on the street for over twenty years. I've woken up in the morning with six inches of snow covering my sleeping bag. I know what homeless is, okay? No politicians came yesterday. No media came. No one wants to cover anything about homeless people any more. It brings me down, I've been so sad. Another person died that shouldn't have been on the streets.

We recently had a big Hunger March in Toronto that I spoke at. Why were we marching? You can't live on $520 a month when a room costs $450. Anyone who tells you there are no hungry people in Canada – they're insane.

All my friends are dying and they're all younger than me. I miss Brian the most. I was with him when he died. We had panned enough money to splurge and get a hotel room for the night. It was $80 for two people. We had a few beers, watched TV for the first time in a while. It was December 20th. In the morning I woke up and he had died in his sleep. I called his parents in Atikokan to tell them. I learned from the coroner that a blood vessel had broken in his brain.

Just up the street, up Sherbourne, there are two vacant houses. Why can't they be turned into affordable housing? We need affordable housing, subsidized housing, because whether you're on social assistance or not, it's hard for most people to afford even a one bedroom apartment – $800 to $900 a month! So what do we need? Affordable housing! When do we need it? NOW! Not sixteen years from now, because people are going to be dying on the streets, so what can we do? We have to try to have rallies where we speak out.

Five years from now I hope I still have my place where I can stay. I hope I can walk around the streets and it's safe. I hope for a city where there will be affordable housing, where the deaths have stopped, where even poor people can afford to do things like go up the CN Tower, have enough food to eat, afford a decent apartment.

I think my best quality is my openness and my friendliness and my knowledge from having learned on the street, and the ways I can help people out. I just love helping people out. I feel good about my role, fighting for the homeless. I'll keep speaking out.

I miss PEI. I think I might retire and go back there. I'd like to be near my mom. I want to make sure I can see her as much as I can. It's just something I've got to do. I've got to see my mom.

CHAPTER 8

JAMES KAGOSHIMA

WISE GUIDE

James telling Crime Commissioner Jim Brown why people squeegee, 1998

James died before I even had the idea for this book. But he is the reason for it. He was grabbed away so quickly. It taught me that I'd better figure out a way to honour some of the amazing homeless activists with whom I do this work.

Here is James's story, in my words.

– Cathy

SINCE I'M A STREET NURSE, MANY PEOPLE THINK THAT THE HOME-less people I know, literally sleep on the street, on a sidewalk or subway grate, or under a bridge, or maybe live in a homeless shelter. Well, James Kagoshima did all of the above at various points in his life. In fact, on November 26th, 2003, Toronto cops gave him one of many tickets for "dwelling in a park." In this case it was for dwelling in "Cloud Gardens" without a permit.

However, I mostly remember James upright, not lying on a grate. I remember him pounding the pavement giving out sleeping bags, knocking at our Toronto Disaster Relief Committee office door, asking for more leaflets and "1%" buttons to give out to homeless people. I remember him striding into our TDRC general members' meeting on a Thursday night, looking extremely handsome, wearing a bright yellow Gore-Tex coat, bright eyed and ready to jump into the agenda. He was our eyes and ears on the street, spreading the word of the "1%" campaign to homeless people, and at the same time reporting back to us, far too often, the news of deaths of his homeless comrades. Tanya Gulliver from the Church of the Holy Trinity says, "I'd be greeted with the efficiency of a newscaster delivering me details about some important issue or recent death. He'd often come in wanting the death list, so he could go agitate somewhere, or so he could convince an agency to check their records."

I first laid eyes on James Kagoshima at a National Housing Day rally, on November 22nd, 2001, outside of Toronto's City Hall. He was in the front row, fully appreciating the live music and speeches coming from the stage. To say James was charismatic, is an understatement. I remember being on stage trying to speak to the crowd, and he just kept heckling me about housing, but in a fun and silly way, laughing and chanting slogans the entire time. He demanded my attention and pretty much continued to do so in the years to come.

He never let me forget that we met on National Housing Day. It was the beginning of a relationship based on our mutual interest – ending homelessness by making politicians accountable. We had a seemingly sixth-sense way of understanding and knowing each other.

James firmly held the politicians accountable. In the fall of 2000 James spoke at the conclusion of a City Council committee meeting where homeless advocates had come forward to press the politicians to respond to homelessness as an emergency. He startled the councillors by pointing out that while they were debating the issue inside a warm building, he had come to talk to them from outside at Nathan Phillips Square, where he had slept the night before. As Tanya recalls, "He made the most eloquent plea about why there should be a state of emergency declared. Even when challenged by a right-wing councillor who claimed that homeless people wanted to stay outside, he just threw it back. He was not intimidated."

There are so many reasons someone like James would still sleep outside: no shelter beds available; a growing intolerance of the conditions inside; and simply being an adult and not wanting rules like curfews. I'm reminded of a phrase in one of his favourite books – *Runaway*, by Evelyn Lau: "I'd rather be living on the streets, standing in puddles of glistening black and neon – at least I'd be free." James loaned me his copy to read.

There are many qualities associated with James:

Creativity. I'm told that when he thought TDRC needed banners, he "borrowed" some sheets from St. Michael's Hospital to make them.

Hopefulness. During the last municipal election, he hounded and pestered fellow Seaton House residents to make sure they voted.

Determination. I remember him at many housing rallies, press conferences, and homeless vigils, sometimes quite ill. I don't know how he made it sometimes. He must have just collapsed once he got back to his shelter bed.

Kindness. Tanya Gulliver says, "He was kind. I never heard him put anyone down unless they were a politician. But boy did he hate politicians who weren't willing to get to work on the issue. He would often seize the microphone at the Homeless Vigils so that he could rant about the inactivity of one sector of the government."

Unique to our relationship was a way of knowing what each other was thinking or needing. I was often confused when I didn't understand what James was saying, but had an intuitive understanding of his intent. Similarly, I felt he could often second-guess me, seemingly knowing what I was thinking or struggling with. Could he read my mind? It often felt like it.

I was never James's nurse. We were more like colleagues. This was his decision. But I still worried about his health. I knew he had many serious health problems, including a tumour in his brain. Several years later when he was incapacitated and confined to a wheelchair in the Seaton House Annex – a harm reduction program in a men's homeless shelter – James agreed

The ticket that police gave James for the crime of sleeping in a park, 2003

that I could discuss his medical care with his physician, Dr. Tomislav Svoboda. Tomislav told me he had decided to treat James aggressively, to do everything he could to get him out of the wheelchair. This worked because James had exceptional stamina and was determined to fight his health problems so he could, in turn, fight homelessness. Before long, he was walking again and speaking out.

Tomislav remembers James's struggle to get well:

> I remember James wanting to get better and to be healthy, and that was a priority for him and, I remember seeing him active. When his friend Leo Cyrenne died, I think James was there and going around with a petition. I remember being impressed that he was actively involved. I didn't know these two worlds of James. I just had the pleasure of working with him in the Annex and he definitely struck me as a person who was motivated, but who had difficulties with his health that he was struggling with. I remember having the feeling that he was a much bigger person than the one I was looking at, that he extended beyond the moment in time when I was looking at him.

In early January 2004, James, still a bit weak, and I took a taxi to a TDRC press conference outside of the Fort York armouries. James had written a speech and it was clear that, although TDRC had not asked him to be a speaker, he *would* be speaking. The Fort York armoury, a federal building, was being used that winter as an emergency shelter, but the federal government was terminating the arrangement with the City and was planning to force homeless people out.

At the press conference, James made his disgust with the federal government clear in his remarks:

> Can I say I am proud to have been an ex-soldier of 3PPCLI [Princess Patricia's Canadian Light Infantry]? The airborne has disgraced the uniform, myself – James Leo Jacobs (his birth name) – and everybody else. Peacekeepers around the world? It's another international disgrace. Thanks, [Paul] Martin.

As if the action had been scripted, James impatiently threw his hat down on the ground, stomped on it, and walked away. I later learned from his speaking

James, on right, at friend Leo's memorial, 2004

notes that this drama was indeed scripted. This event led to a big victory. The feds backed down and postponed the eviction date. This bought time for the City to negotiate a deal with the owner of an empty building, once used as a nursing student residence, to use it for emergency shelter during the remainder of the winter. As an even sweeter victory, that same building has now been turned into affordable housing.

James reached out to many of his brothers and sisters on the street – people I could never have reached. He brought them sleeping bags, food, and friendship. At the same time, he did what I call "upstream" advocacy. Art Manuel, of the Seaton House Annex, remembers James speaking to mayoral candidate David Miller when he came to tour the Annex: "James was out there with a message that we need more harm reduction programs and we need to have more support around this. This is good work." James was always a sophisticated advocate and his political follow-through was impeccable. He was thrilled when David Miller was elected Mayor, and at a TDRC press conference declared Miller good

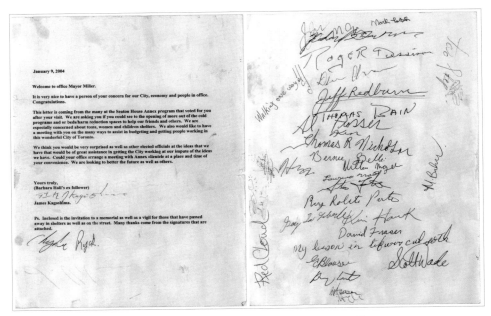

Sample of the signatures that James collected calling for Mayor David Miller to open more shelters, 2004

enough to be prime minister. Several months later he attached a copy of over a hundred signatures to a letter to the mayor:

> Welcome to office, Mayor Miller.
>
> It's very nice to have a person of your concern for our City, economy, and people, in office. Congratulations.
>
> This letter is coming from the many at the Seaton House Annex program that voted for you after your visit. We are asking you if you could see to the opening of more out of the cold programs and or beds/harm reduction spaces to help our friends and others. We are especially concerned about teens, women, and children shelters.

Again showing the kind of follow-through many advocates could learn from, he ended with:

Could your office arrange a meeting with Annex clientele at a place and time of your convenience? P.S. Enclosed is the invitation to a memorial as well as a vigil for those that have passed away in shelters as well as on the street. Many thanks come from the signatures that are attached.

Ironically, James himself would be remembered at the same vigil, only two months later.

James almost got his wish to spend time with Mayor Miller. On Friday, February 13th, 2004, just days before he died, James was to join me on a nighttime walkabout with the mayor. James would introduce the mayor to homeless people sleeping outside, and outline his own solutions to homelessness. James didn't show up. I felt a twinge of worry but suppressed it. There were many reasons he might not have made it. Little did I know…

On Tuesday, February 17th, I woke, and for reasons not clear to me and which I still can't explain, I called my colleague Michael Shapcott to cancel a morning meeting with him. I had a nagging feeling that I was supposed to go to St. Michael's Hospital, although I wasn't sure why. I couldn't think of anyone I knew in hospital at the time.

Then, around 11 A.M., Art Manuel, from Seaton House, called me. "Cathy, I've got bad news." He told me James was in ICU, not doing well. It didn't look good. Did I know how to reach family?

Well, I knew what those words meant. I grabbed a cab and headed to St. Mike's.

James wasn't conscious, but I spoke to him and told him how brave he was and how much we loved him. I felt quite out of place in the high-tech space – there were lots of tubes, whose purpose I didn't even know, going into James. Nurses were looking at me with curiosity. My memories of what happens to homeless people once they're in hospital flooded into my mind. How could I explain to the ICU nurses that the man lying there was an activist, a great man? I timidly asked them if I could pin a "1%" button on his gown, and did.

Special Motion, Toronto City Council, March 1st, 2004

NOTICE OF MOTION

Moved by: Mayor David Miller

Seconded by: Councillor Olivia Chow

WHEREAS the Mayor and Members of Toronto City Council are deeply saddened to learn of the sudden passing of James (Jacobs) Kagoshima on February 17, 2004; and

WHEREAS at the time of his death, James Kagoshima lived at Seaton House and was well known to the homeless community; and

WHEREAS he was a proud aboriginal man from Northern Ontario who spent much of his time working on the issues of homelessness and fighting injustice; and

WHEREAS he spoke several times to City Council and its committees about his concerns and most recently was involved in encouraging the city to keep the armouries open to house the homeless; and

WHEREAS James Kagoshima wanted his death to be remembered as much as his life;

NOW THEREFORE, BE IT RESOLVED THAT the City Clerk be directed to convey, on behalf of Members of City Council, our sincere sympathy to members of his family, and to members of the homeless community through the Toronto Disaster Relief Committee.

I learned that family had been contacted and had visited James. Other friends and Seaton House staff visited him too. The difficult decision of removing life supports was made by family. James was forty-one.

I later learned that the day after our scheduled walk with the mayor, James had walked himself into the St. Mike's Emergency Department, and then rapidly deteriorated. He died one week before Mayor Miller's Summit on Housing and Homelessness, where without doubt James would have made an impression.

James knew how tenuous life was. In 2003 he organized a large memorial for his friend Leo Cyrenne, who had died homeless. On that day, ten names of homeless people were added to the Memorial Board at the Church of the Holy Trinity. Immediately following that service James rushed back to Seaton House for yet another memorial for another man. James often said that he would be next.

Yet, when that same year a rumour circulated that James had died, he laughed, and said that in death, as in life, he wanted to have a big impact. He just became more precious to us.

In recent weeks James had talked a lot about rejoining his wife and daughter in Japan. James, an Ojibway by birth, loved his wife Miwako so much that he took on her Japanese name Kagoshima. They met when both were Frontiers Foundation volunteers building housing in the Northwest Territories.

Notice of the memorial for James, 2004

James was born James Moreau Jacobs. He was taken from his native mother when he was very little and was bounced around a number of foster homes until he was about eight. When he was adopted as a young boy he became Jim Buchanan, and later when he moved in with the son of one of his foster parents he became Jim Mahon.

A memorial celebrating his life was held at the Church of the Holy Trinity, the place where James himself had often remembered fallen comrades. Members of his family, homeless people, Seaton House staff, leaders from faith communities, housing activists, non-profit housing builders, and university students attended. To quote Catherine Dunphy from the *Toronto Star*, "He fought homelessness from the front lines for another reason: He lived it."

Speech by Frank Mahon at Memorial for James Kagoshima, Church of the Holy Trinity, Toronto, March 9th, 2004

When someone who has always been a part of your life passes away, you reflect on all of the good things about that person, and any difficulties you may have had, tend to seem trivial. Jim died at the age of forty-one. Some knew him for a short period. Others like my family knew him for the majority of his life. Jim came into our lives at the age of two, a cute little bundle of curiosity ready to take on the world and everything it could throw at him. And the world did throw many things his way. Jim struggled with alcohol. He struggled with drugs. He also struggled with who he was and what his place in the world might be. Jim struggled to be who he finally became, but one thing that was never in doubt – he was a good soul. The caring and compassion he showed to others was always there.

One day last month Lois was listening to a CBC radio program. The guests were inner-city children talking about their lives. One child made a profound statement: "Everybody is somebody to somebody." To everybody here today, Jim was some-body. To some he was a son, a friend, an advocate, or to some of you he may just have been the guy that brought you a blanket on a cold night. To me and my family he was someone whom we will always love and of whom we will always be proud. He made a difference in the world.

In coming here today we want to celebrate Jim's life and also share specific memories of him so that everyone can truly understand who he was. To me, my wife, and our family, Jim was a two-year-old who, when he saw snow for the first time and it got on his boots, he brushed it off with his little hand and wanted to be picked up. He was the little boy who would grab my hand and squeeze so tight. You couldn't help but fall in love with him. He went camping with our family, he won a National Bowling Championship in Thunder Bay when he was thirteen years old. He did so many things.

He dropped out of high school, but in his late twenties he returned to get his high school diploma. He was so proud of this, he mailed it to us to prove he had done it! Jim wanted to be "book" educated but he learned so much more and became so wise through the experience of life. Jim was an artist. Each day I look at the two pictures he did for me which hang in my office. Jim was a brother to our sons Ryan and Devon. They will dearly miss him.

Jim, to others you are that kind soul who gave them a blanket. You are the young man who built houses for the needy in the Northwest Territories. You were the husband who loved his wife dearly and you were the father who was so very proud of your daughter. Rayuka is eight years old and lives in Japan. Jim will live on in her.

You had a difficult time saying "I love you," but the little crocodile that you gave me at Christmas one year said it all: "I love you and that's no croc!" Jim we all love you and miss you. We will hold your memory near... "and that's no croc."

Jim felt everyone was responsible for each other, that we all hold a spot in making life a better place for everyone. I know Jim is here in spirit, but if he were here in person I'm sure he would agree that his life, like everyone's, had significant meaning. He was "SOMEBODY."

In closing, think of each other with love. Always support and guide one another. On Jim's behalf I would like to leave you with this verse which could have been his creed to live by:

DON'T WALK IN FRONT OF ME, I MAY NOT FOLLOW

DON'T WALK BEHIND ME, I MAY NOT LEAD

JUST WALK BESIDE ME, AND BE MY FRIEND!

Gladys, thank you so much for sharing your son with us, we are all better people because of that experience.

James honoured homeless people, men, women, and children. He honoured the Seaton House shelter staff that cared for him deeply. He honoured Mother Earth.

Mostly, he honoured the right for every person in Canada to have a home.

CHAPTER 9

KEVIN CLARKE

STREET POLITICIAN

Kevin, protesting his exclusion from mayoralty debate, University of Toronto, 2006

I was asked to write a profile of a homeless person for Toronto's *Eye Weekly*.

The following is adapted from the original piece, which appeared in May 2005.

– Cathy

IF THERE'S ONE THING I'VE LEARNED AFTER SEVENTEEN YEARS AS a street nurse, it's that there's no such thing as a typical homeless person. The stereotype of a man lying prone on a sidewalk or heating grate, has never fit with the people I knew to be homeless. Over the years I've met artists, engineers, truckers, hydro workers, highly skilled steelworkers, professionals like police officers and nurses, war vets and, of course, families. Some ended up living on those grates, but mostly I saw people upright, struggling 24/7 to survive, caught in a labyrinth to find food, shelter, health care.

Then there's Kevin Clarke. Kevin became homeless in 1998, after his small auto business failed. He's lived on the street, literally, since then.

I'm sure it's all more complicated than that, but what's important is who he is now and where he's headed.

Kevin is perhaps one of the most recognized homeless people on Toronto's downtown streets. (I'm convinced that one of the homeless characters on the CBC TV show *This Is Wonderland* is modelled after Kevin.) Whether it's at Bay and Adelaide, or outside the Air Canada Centre, if you don't notice Kevin in his dramatic attire (what he calls his "robes"), you hear him – singing, rhythmically speaking out, or preaching (great vocal cords – when does he breathe?!). Kevin is an apostle, the spreader of the faith that each person is a treasure, worthy of respect, love, *and* housing. He preaches on abuse of authority, the role individuals can play in curbing the path of social decay, through acceptance, and the importance of homes, rather than services that encourage dependency. That's a mouthful, and it's how he talks. He's literally trying to curb homelessness from the curb by changing attitudes and talking about human rights. The right to respect. The right to housing.

I phone Kevin at the Parkdale Activity Recreation Centre (PARC), a popular and crowded west-end drop-in centre where he spends time, to arrange an interview. He was there to use the free phone and excitedly tells me he has just gotten a call back from City Councillor Case Ootes. Kevin has been busy, canvassing councillors, urging them to vote against the City's proposed by-law to make it illegal for homeless people to sleep outside the City Hall. It's quite possible he's working harder on this issue than most front-line advocates.

Kevin suggests we meet at a restaurant called the True Love Café. It's located at the heart of Toronto's homeless disaster, at Sherbourne and Dundas. Over the years the restaurant has had a variety of owners and menus, usually consisting of grilled cheese, burgers, and fries. It was once George's Spaghetti House, a Toronto landmark known for its nighttime jazz. I'm surprised to see it converted into what appears to be an internet café, complete with a mix of sofas and lounge chairs, stuffed toys and teddy bears, and an expanded menu that includes a "Garden of Eden" salad, deli sandwiches, French toast, and herbal teas.

When I arrive at True Love, Kevin is hunkered down over one of the free computers, and to my surprise is checking his e-mail. He was hoping to have enough time to write a presentation for the City's Policy and Finance Committee, on the City's controversial "From Streets into Homes" report. Not only is Kevin engaged in what's going on at City Hall, he's also an active member of the Toronto Disaster Relief Committee, and plans to be at the group's meeting at All Saints Church, just across the street, immediately following our meeting.

Speech by Kevin Clarke, at Safe Park, 1999

Homelessness is madness and Toronto will never be a great city, and Ontario will never be a great province, and Canada will never be a great country, until you take care of the poor and the needy. The legacy of any great city, any great province, and any great country, is that it takes care of the poor and the needy so that everyone has the right to enjoy the fruits of life.

Today Kevin is wearing his "robes": a long flowing white tunic, a shawl, and a headdress with a yellow headband. When I ask him why, he flashes a huge grin and patiently explains: first, because they are warm (it's chilly out when we speak), and second, because when he encounters kids, it puts a smile on their face. As he says, "I dress the way I dress because it's the way I am. Some days I wear red – the colour of humanity."

Kevin tells me that this afternoon he just came from Bay and Adelaide, where he used to live on the sidewalk for three and a half years. He describes a connection with people there, and members of the business community telling him "it's good to see you back." He says they were the best two hours of his life. BAY Street, he points out stands for "Buy All You," meaning it's the financial district. ADELAIDE, on the other hand, is a one-way street: "All Deeds Enable Love And Is Decided Equally," and that's the street closest to Kevin's own personal direction. For two straight hours Kevin did just what he used to do at Bay and Adelaide when he lived there – spoke out and sang from his heart to passersby.

Why is Kevin so happy today? Well, one reason is he's just gotten housing – thanks to what he refers to as the "Koyama method," a humorous but respectful reference to Danielle Koyama, an activist with the Toronto Disaster Relief Committee who, on her own time, assisted and supported Kevin in finding housing. According to Kevin, the "Koyama method" is all about "working with people as individuals, keeping a focus on meeting their needs, not on their problems." Kevin now lives in a bachelor apartment in Parkdale. In the social-worky world of homelessness, homeless people sometimes get labelled as "hard to house." I suspect Kevin would have been categorized as such. Despite this label, and not unlike the hundred at Tent City who got housed after their waterfront eviction, Kevin is quite happy to have housing. Neither Kevin nor the Tent City hundred have begged to go back to the street – countering the prevailing myth that people "choose" to sleep outside, and to not go into a shelter. Kevin recently stayed outside and slept on a grate, but only to remind himself of the experience, to be reassociated with the issues, to refuel his ability to speak the truth.

Kevin in park in Parkdale, 2005

I still don't understand how people like Kevin survive sleeping outside for years and remain whole. I ask him to tell me in practical terms how he stayed warm and didn't get hurt or die. Although he makes references to the aches and pains he feels "day by day in his bones" – likely an outcome of the cold and damp, Kevin claims that his survival, both physical and emotional, depended on people who interacted with him as a person, offering him food, conversation, supplies, and respect, not the City enforcers who kept moving him along.

Kevin will be forty-one on March 21st, the first day of spring, the day when he poetically claims "the beauty begins." He came to Canada from St. Anne's, Jamaica, when he was eleven, to join his hard-working mother, Millicent. He speaks lovingly of his mother, whom he has recently visited in hospital. When I spoke to Millicent she took great pains to explain to me that she simply can't understand why her son was homeless for so many years. She described searching for him when he fell off her radar for a while, and being surprised that so many people knew and cared about her son. She's clearly relieved that he's alive and that he's now in housing after so many years. She's happy to have regular contact with him – proudly telling me how she made him lasagna last night when he came by for a visit.

Not unlike other homeless people, Kevin has a number of talents and interests. During a co-op course in his last year of high school, he taught math and phys-ed to Grade 5 kids in a Toronto public school, and clearly misses "their laughter, and the message of joy that a child sends." When I ask Millicent to tell me something special about her son, she immediately says, "He loves children."

Kevin is supremely interested in politics. So what does he think of how Toronto is handling the homeless situation? He considers the ban on sleeping at Nathan Phillips Square to be simply an extension of what already happens to homeless people on the streets and in the parks. Kevin is no stranger to the City's harassment of the homeless. He thinks he may be the person most arrested in the city for being homeless – a minimum of thirty-eight times according to a document he prepared for his own defence in one of his trials. In most cases he was imprisoned and forced to go through the judicial process, only to have charges withdrawn or dismissed. He knows by their names and departments the city workers who, over the years, have "visited" him "more than many times" to move him along. Kevin refers to the Charter of Rights and asks, "What is our responsibility as individuals, as a city? We have a responsibility to provide for people's basic needs." He believes the City must put a hold on this abandonment of homeless people, and the forced movement of the homeless by police and City workers.

Kevin cautions that, since homelessness has become such a prominent issue, we haven't heard much about unemployment, or about the welfare system. His goal is to stem the path of homelessness, dealing with the obstacles that lead people there.

If you get the sense that Kevin is politically engaged, you're right, in more ways than one. Kevin provides me with a dizzying list of elections he's run in. He's a determined campaigner, having faced politicians like David Miller, Gerard Kennedy, and Jane Pitfield.

From 1994 to 1997 he did what he believes no man in the history of Canada has ever done: he ran for office in three different elections at all three levels of government. In 1994 he faced a municipal mayor (Michael Prue); in 1995 a provincial premier (Bob Rae); and in 1997 a federal MP (Dennis Mills). Kevin recently abandoned his plan to run in a further federal election. It was going to be hard to come up with the deposit, but he also decided to build himself up to be a serious threat for the mayor's job.

Kevin is still running, using every opportunity he can to make passionate political speeches. At the TDRC meeting later that night Kevin gives a motivational speech, not unlike an evangelical preacher, directed to a group of nursing students in the front row, stressing how we all must engage people in the fight to protect homeless people. Several weeks later at a rally at All Saints Church that will head to City Council chambers for a protest, he speaks to a crowd of his peers – fellow users of the drop-in centre – about challenging the mayor for planning to make it illegal to be homeless outside the City Hall. I wonder how Kevin's peers would react to him. It's not often that one of their own gets to speak to them, as a leader, at the microphone. I'm moved by the number of homeless people who quietly approach him to shake his hand and say, "Good speech."

I too tell Kevin what a great speech he gave. He shrugs and grins: "I believe I do something to homelessness that no one else does. I put people's focus on the homeless individual as being just like themselves. Homeless people are people first."

His ability to reach people extends beyond people he encounters on the street. Kevin is also an actor, and recently performed with Mixed Company. Director Simon Malbogat is known around the world for his work in what some call "the theatre of the oppressed."

I recently saw Kevin perform with Mixed Company – the occasion was a twenty-four hour vigil held at the Homeless Memorial. The play was powerful, with scenes that addressed police violence, public complacency, and the

Address to Toronto City Council, by Kevin Clarke, January 31st, 2006

Kevin recently applied to be appointed by City Council to replace Olivia Chow in Ward 20, after her election to the House of Commons. The following are excerpts from his address to City Council on January 31st, 2006. The speech was delivered with the rhythm and passion of a southern preacher.

– Cathy

In this city we have extreme problems, extreme problems with gun violence – number one. As your Councillor in Ward 20, I will inspire hope in the young people, not only in Ward 20, but all across the city. I will show them that I came from being an ex-con, from being a homeless man, to where I was given the equal opportunity. I will show them that Council was not racist, and this Council did not say, "You're just homeless, you're a bum." This Council will say, "Mr. Clarke, you went from sleeping under a bridge, you came from eating out of garbage cans, you came from being a homeless man, you came from being the most arrested homeless man (wrongly!)."

You came to this Council and you gave us your qualifications and we gave you the opportunity because you deserved it.

I'm here to say it's not about character. It's not about character, it's about charity. My character is about feeding the hungry. You ask any one in this city – I will never pass a man, a woman, or a child, who is hungry, without giving them food.

My character is to be a friend to the lonely. I am looking forward to feeding the hungry in Ward 20. I am looking forward to walking the streets day and night and seeing that the homeless have an opportunity. I am looking forward to being a friend to the lonely. Thank you.

institutionalization of homelessness. Kevin was great. As he walked away, he caught a pigeon in his hands and threw it up in the air. It was like magic.

In a quieter moment I ask Kevin what he hopes for. He replies more seriously, "I'm a realist but I'm also a dreamer. I would like to see a smile on all the people that I pass by. I would like to see children playing in the parks. I'd like to see more stories in the media about people helping seniors cross the street, young children excelling in their school work, and playing sports. I'd like to see homelessness become extinct. I believe homelessness in the City is an issue that has been passed down to the municipality by the federal government."

Kevin proclaims that his overall goal in life is to spread love, and reminds me that it's no accident we're meeting at the True Love Café. In a subsequent e-mail to me he writes, "God bless, put the kids first, and inspire hope in all."

And always practical, he points to the empty tin can on the ground beside his feet where he's accepting donations so he can buy this week's IGA chicken special. I drop some money in. Living on welfare and paying rent in the private housing market doesn't leave you a lot left for food.

CHAPTER 10

BONNIE AND KERRE BRIGGS

TALENTED DUO

Bonnie and Kerre participating in the Homeless Memorial, 2006

They're just always there. Or at least one of them – Bonnie or Kerre. At every single meeting, rally, march, demonstration, fundraiser, memorial, or conference that has *anything* to do with homelessness or housing – they are there. And you always know they're there because they play a big part in whatever is going on. Whether it's Kerre, at the recent National Homelessness Conference, speaking in French at the microphone to make the francophone Quebeckers feel welcome, or Bonnie speaking out at the more formal City Hall Homeless Advisory Committee, on the rights of homeless couples, they each have a commanding presence. It has occurred to me that they've been doing this work at least as long as I have. They've been homeless, but they've more than just survived their own homelessness. They've carried their personal fight for a home onto a bigger stage. They've continued their advocacy work facing enormous challenges: not-so-stable housing, hunger, not enough money to live on, health problems, and, I'm sad to say, discriminatory attitudes within the very social justice movement they've come to be part of.

Yet somehow, this couple, who on first glance seem polar opposites, have sustained each other and have maintained a steadfast belief in the valuable role they play fighting for homeless people's right to housing.

– Cathy

ON MEETING

Kerre: We met at a dance in Kleinberg at the Binder Twine Festival. There was a big flatbed truck, with a blues rock band – the Back Beats – playing on it, in the parking lot of the gas station. Neither one of us was looking at the time.

Bonnie: I had on this old granny gown, it was a long, long dress with puff sleeves and a bow at the back. Friends had made it for me. If you came in costume, you'd get in for free. He asked me for a dance.

K: Now, I'm a blues musician, so I'd decided to go to Kleinberg with my harmonicas to try to sit in and play with these guys. Now, Bonnie mentions the granny gown, that's really significant, because I turn around and see her, she's dancing by herself, she had long blonde hair at the time. I see this person dancing by herself! Now, Kleinberg is famous for some pretty unique Canadian icons such as the McMichael Collection of the Group of Seven. Pierre Berton is from there too. Then, I see Bonnie, and I thought, she's *really* an individual, I've got to meet her.

B: I was a half a mile from the nearest bus and would've had to hitchhike home....

K: So at the end of the night, I drove her home and introduced her to my dad. I figured that's the end of that, because she was seeing someone else at the time. But a couple of weeks later she showed up at my dad's house and said to me, "Hi, do you want to go to a movie?"

B: We got married in 1983, exactly one year from the day we met. We were married in a church in a place called New Toronto, or Mimico. I had the white gown, the whole thing. We've been married twenty-two years September 11th – not knowing that September 11 was going to be that infamous date many years later.

K: We got married in a Ukrainian Orthodox church because it was most in line with what I believed in. Her family are Protestants, I grew up Catholic. They wanted to be rid of me ASAP.

ON GROWING UP

B: I was born in Brampton in 1953, but grew up in Willowdale, in Toronto. I spent a number of years travelling back and forth to Florida for vacations. I had rheumatic fever and breathing problems, so the salt air was helpful to me. We moved to Thornhill, and after my adoptive parents died, I lived in Maple with an aunt.

I was adopted when I was about a year old, but I didn't know that most of my life. I found out when I was about twenty-five. The woman who brought me up, who I thought was my mother, was really my aunt. Her sister, who I

400 Too Many

[poem read jointly at twenty-four-hour vigil, August 9th, 2005]

We begin attempting to name and remember

Those who have fallen on the street.

James with his red pants and good friend Ryck.

June with her green Tourister luggage.

Tom with his gentle spirit.

Janet with her favourite faithful ways.

Edyth with her broken beauty in her wide community.

Lester, a well known regular at the Meeting Place.

Who are the nameless?

The John and Jane Does have increased.

The Coroner is unwilling or forbidden to speak.

Some families live in shame or have divorced the lost one long, long ago.

Some don't have families.

These anonymous ones are buried in unmarked graves with

No one to plant geraniums.

There is too much suffering and pain.

There is too much that is unknown.

There is too much cover-up.

There is too much spent on Band-Aids rather than on the long-term solutions.

Housing provides dignity and hope.

It has an address and a potential to have a phone number.

It offers a permanence that not even the best hostel can manage.

We need vigilance, attention, and outrage at the city's short-term expenditures.

We need to speak not only to the politicians but to our friends and companions.

We need to create a groundswell of people clamouring for housing now.

In memory of the 400 who have passed, we need housing and we need it NOW.

May they not have died in vain.

   – Bonnie Briggs and Kerre Briggs

thought was my aunt, was actually my mother. I have two sisters, but one just died a few weeks ago, and I've got a brother. I don't have contact with them. My biological mom has since died.

I just got a letter from my aunt saying that my mother's kids want to get to know me. I haven't seen them for more than fifteen years.

K: I was born in 1956 in Montreal and, considering the state of premature medical technology, by rights I shouldn't be here. I was born two or three months premature and I was three pounds, six ounces. I was pocket-sized. My mom almost died having me. I always say I was like the prototype. I was the first one, then my mom had three more children.

I have a hidden sense of humour. Some people think that when I was born in Quebec, a nurse put some poutine in my Gerber's so that I couldn't taste the puréed carrots, which may have detoured my so-called normal development.

My mom came from a really wealthy family. They were "in sugar" – St. Lawrence, or Redpath. In 1939 Mackenzie King seized my grandfather's assets, like ships, for the war effort, and the story is that he was so upset that he died, in 1942. My grandmother was an artist and created blueprints for designing Lancaster bombers. She ended up putting my mother and her sisters and brother into a convent or an orphanage so she could look for another husband and father for her kids. In 1948 she remarried, the man I knew as my grandfather.

My dad was from an Irish-French background. They were Bouchards when they first came to Canada in the 1600s, when Quebec was called New France. In 1907 my grandfather anglicized his name to Briggs in order to get work. A lot of early 1900 immigrants to North America had to do that. I grew up speaking English at home. The extent of our French was watching *Chez Hélène* on television, except when we were visiting my grandfather and his French-Canadian friends.

I grew up in French-speaking Montreal, an area that was the industrial heartland of the city. I remember hearing the shift whistles at the factories, near the Lachine Canal. My parents moved us to a Montreal suburb – Candiac – and bought a house, but they were somewhat limited by their finances, and their marriage quietly and gradually deteriorated over time. For me, moving to a subdivision in the middle of nowhere was emotionally a big shock, and it kind of screwed me up. At school, I had the crap kicked out of me for seven years. I was bullied, physically. It felt really competitive and ultimately I never felt I really belonged there. I wanted out.

When my parents split up I ended up living with my dad and moving to Toronto, in 1972. I was about fifteen. So Toronto is like a second home. But it wasn't easy. My dad had a lot of financial and alcohol problems. He was also supporting a second family by then because he had remarried. When I was sixteen I left home and joined the Canadian Army Reserves. My dad is dead now and my mom is still in Candiac. I'm still in touch with her.

ON BECOMING HOMELESS

B: In 1986 we were living in the basement of a house that our landlord had bought without being able to afford it. When he was forced to sell it we were told the new owner wanted us out. We were homeless for a couple of weeks, when we took a place that offered free rent in return for looking after the family's three-year-old autistic child. That didn't work out – it was like *Dennis the Menace*. We had nowhere to go, so we began going to the Relax Inn, near the 400 and Finch, where we could rent rooms by the week, just to get a roof over our heads.

K: That was when we had enough money to do that. I was working at Leon's, a furniture store. Thank god for the Leon family, because they knew what I was going through, and my boss quietly let me have some time off to go look for a place.

On and off we spent nights wandering, looking for a place to stay. Hours of walking and searching, often in York Region. Staying at motels along Highway 7, west of Keele.

B: There was a lot of discrimination. Back then, landlords only wanted to rent to one person, not a couple. And when we tried to get into a shelter they wouldn't take us because we didn't have kids. Our marriage was almost at the breaking point. It was at the point where we couldn't stand each other. We fought over the smallest things.

K: In some ways, I saw the homeless crisis coming. I'd been watching the situation develop since the mid '70s. People were buying up rooming houses, especially in places like the Annex and Cabbagetown in Toronto, and turning them into single-family homes. Tenants were put out on the street. Gentrification. That affordable housing was lost and was not replaced, and the government did nothing about it for ten to fifteen years. I remember saying to a Global TV reporter that if nothing was done, we were going to have a huge housing crisis. Back then, for every thousand units in Toronto, only one was available to rent. People would line up to look at that one place, and the landlord would pick who to give it to based on how they looked.

I know people who want to forget about that experience. One of Mel Lastman's former assistants told me he'd been homeless and he wanted to forget about it. The thing is, truthfully, being homeless and every night having to find a different place just to sleep is horrifying.

B: We stayed in the back of a car for about a week, in bus shelters, in the visitors lounge at Humber Memorial Hospital, in a laundromat, even on the roof of a four-storey building. We did this for about a three-month period. Always basically living by our wits. Kerre had survival training from the Boy Scouts and the Canadian Army and he coupled those skills with his personality and used them to keep us alive in a very dangerous situation. One night we were sleeping in a hallway in an apartment building and Kerre had to talk the cops out of arresting us for trespassing. After that Kerre put me into a women's shelter – Robertson House – because I wasn't sleeping or eating right. Kerre was working full-time then. I stayed at other women's shelters too: Street Haven, Rendu, Evangeline.

K: There was so much pressure. It almost caused us to split up. Being separated from each other took a toll on our marriage. But I thought Bonnie should be in a shelter for her own safety. I went and lived in an abandoned car in north Toronto, a ten-minute walk from my work. I used a subway locker to keep my clothes and belongings safe. I never missed a day of work and I was never late. Nobody knew I was living in a Toronado, up on blocks, except the guys that would be slowly stripping the car. One day the guy knocked

DYING FOR A HOME

on the window and said, "Hey man, how are you, can we have the steering wheel now?"

B: Somehow Kerre was able to perform his job to his usual high standards during all this time. He was never late, never missed a day of work, and often worked overtime. Often, all he could afford to eat were potato chips, coffee, and doughnuts. Eventually I got a union job and we were also able to find some places to live. We lived with some friends for a while, about seven of us in a tiny apartment. People were sleeping on the floor in the living room. But landlords still didn't want to rent to a couple. Then we moved to Maple, out of the city for awhile.

K: We were really only homeless for that one big episode until Mel Lastman, who was mayor of North York in 1988, made moves to get rid of rooming houses. Our landlord freaked and told us we had to leave. He evicted us. We couch-surfed with friends for about six months. Then we went back to the Relax Inn for a few months, and then we came in "for a landing" at the place we live now.

We got the place we're in now because the house was abandoned in a neighbourhood I had known since 1960. I said to the landlord that I would fix the place up, cut the lawn, etc., if he would let us move in.

B: I've been living in Parkdale since about 1995. Kerre moved here in 2001. It's a tiny one bedroom apartment in a three-storey building with a nice balcony. Our rent is $529 plus hydro.

Our oven hadn't worked since before last Christmas. We had no oven to cook our turkey in, a few Christmases ago, only three burners worked, but it's working now. We have a huge hole in the ceiling in the bathroom. The bathroom cabinets are hanging by one hinge, we need a new lock on the back door, plus various other things. But they'll get fixed.

ON FOOD

B: We still rely on the food bank, but not as much. We receive a special diet allowance now on our cheque. It means we can go to the IGA and spend eighty bucks on food and not worry about it. It means we can have meat more than once a month, and fresh vegetables. I can now buy broccoli and cauliflower. I

Love Me, Love Me Not

Liberals, Conservatives, and the
    Greens,
Love me, love me not.
The Feds, the Province, the City,
Love me, love me not.
With each old promise unfulfilled,
A petal drops, love unfulfilled.
Love me, love me not,
For those we name on this cold day.
The hope has fled,
For a soft, safe bed.
The silent conspiracy of these
    Governments three,
Deepens the lack of dignity.
The souls left out are bruised and
    shattered,
Like the lepers of yore.

The black slaves in the south,
They witness to us all, most often with
    silent and vacant eyes,
That our Governments have not
    produced equality or housing
    for all.
Love me seems to mean
Food banks, shelters, Out of the Cold,
Drop-ins, day programs, workers who
    often seem out of touch.
They each provide,
With all of their rules.
A short time in, a place to stay.
But all of the workers
Who joined to help
Know the limits of their offerings,
And begin to know

can buy the kind of cereal I like, and not have to eat Cheerios because that's what they're giving out at the food bank. Last week we went to the Scott Mission and got food and clothes. Going to food banks is very stressful. If you can go out and buy your own food, it's really so much better.

K: It's still about survival. Up until recently we had about $20 to $30 left for food after paying our rent and bills. If it weren't for food banks I wouldn't be here right now.

B: We're all set for Christmas. Friends are coming over and our food is all ordered from a catalogue that specializes in hampers. They deliver it right to you. We're also getting a food hamper for the cats. The food lasts for weeks.

That beneath the transitions
From place to place, is a need for
    housing
That transcends their power.
Love must shout from roof top and
    grate,
"Housing is basic, something we
    all need."
To move ahead, one needs some skill,
A safe place to sleep.
A caring bud, a loving brother.
One needs an address,
A door to lock,
And even a little furry cat.
These are the goals.
And the showing of love
That we can find, my friends,

We need to work.
That "1 %,"
And bring homelessness to an end.
So, love your best,
And plan to win.
We can change the homeless plight.
Our hearts and commitment and
    repeated cries
Create a place for a turning tide.
Love me, love me not,
The children's chanting says.
But love me deep,
Love me true,
Brings the change we want for me
    and you.
    – Bonnie Briggs and Sara Boyles
    (Feb. 14, 2006)

ON THEIR HEALTH

K: Well, I have PTSD [post-traumatic stress disorder].

B: We! I'm still waiting to hear from Disability to see if my application is approved. It's my third application. This last application has been in for six months. If I receive Disability then I can get a hearing aid. I'm almost deaf in my left ear and my right ear is super-sensitive to high-pitched sounds. I had surgery when I was a kid, at White Memorial Hospital in Los Angeles. I also have a heart murmur and a leaky valve from rheumatic fever.

K: My health is good, although I'm told that I had several small strokes in 2000. I had been working sixteen-hour shifts for twenty-five days straight.

One day my boss took one look at me and sent me home, and then I ended up in Mount Sinai. I have severe arthritis and I'm seeing a neurologist now to investigate my tremors. I'm worried because I have had a concussion. My head has sometimes been used as a crash helmet since I was a kid. I've just been diagnosed with hyperthyroidism and have started medication for that. I had a lot of symptoms – a tremor, heart palpitations, I was tired all the time, and my eyes were kind of bulging. I'm happy they found out what it was and that it wasn't Parkinson's disease.

B: We're making a home remedy now to keep us healthy – it's a cup of cider vinegar, a cup of honey, and eight garlic cloves. You mix it all up in the blender and then put it in the fridge for five days. Each morning you put two teaspoons in a glass of water and drink it before breakfast. It's not bad.

K: I want to get back to where I'm healthy and I can do the things that I like doing and I'm good at. I don't want to go back to washing dishes, and long sixteen-hour days, seven days a week. That's probably what put me in this condition to begin with.

I have to take an indefinite sabbatical of sorts until I can get my health back. I hope that people will see my absence from housing and homelessness events as something I need to do for my health's sake.

ON FUN AND HOBBIES

B: I've been part of a drumming group for ten years. I love percussion. In the summer we drum every Sunday, outdoors at Sunnyside Park. In the winter, we have what we call a tam-tam, which is a big party – it's a drumming party and we drum and dance, and at New Year's we have a potluck. Dressing up is optional, and it's only $10. It's a helluva lot more fun than spending $100 in the city at a club.

I've just joined another band, called "Loki," and we perform once or twice a month. I love percussion, music, dancing. I like going to see bands. I love old cars, trains, and trucks. I like animals and working on my computer doing web pages. I have a blog now about animals and other creatures. We have two cats, Smokey and Tinker. Tinker is Smokey's father.

K: I've been a blues musician for much of thirty-five years. I play electric guitar, blues harmonica, keyboards. I've played saxophone, percussion. I'm a cartoonist, writer, filmmaker, actor, broadcaster, and I do photography. We're both veteran actors and I've done some improv [Kerre does great Richard Nixon and Jimmy Stewart impersonations – Cathy]. We're in a movie called *JoJo* about homelessness. It's a lot like Don Shebib's *Goin' Down the Road*.

B: We've both had web sites for a long time. I have a web site for my poetry, one about endangered animals, one about drumming, and a couple of others. Kerre's is more on homelessness and activism. We've even written a book of our own. It's called *The Squat*. It's the first of three books that we're going to write.

Bonnie drumming in protest against harassment of street youth, 1998

ON BECOMING AND BEING ACTIVISTS

B: When I was younger, when the *Toronto Telegram* was still publishing, I used to write letters to them about saving old buildings. One of the buildings I was trying to save was the municipal hall in North York. In high school I circulated a petition against animal leg-hold traps. People made fun of me.

We were both homeless in 1987. I was staying at a shelter in 1987 during the International Year of the Homeless and they took a group of us to Ottawa for a conference. I also went to Queen's Park for No Place Like Home, and then I joined the Basic Poverty Action Group. Those are my roots as a housing activist. I thought it was important to get involved. I never knew about homelessness until I was homeless. I never considered that I would ever be homeless, so for me, it's important to do something.

Kerre at Church of the Holy Trinity, 2006

I later learned about the Ontario Coalition Against Poverty [OCAP] and the Toronto Disaster Relief Committee [TDRC]. I just started going to the meetings and rallies. I've just now been asked to join the TDRC Steering Committee. That was pretty amazing. I'm proud of that and hopefully I can contribute due to my experience of being homeless – the things I've gone through.

K: I was more gradually politicized. I'm a true kid of the late '60s. I grew up watching TV and seeing the Cuban missile crisis, JFK, Bobby Kennedy, and then the Martin Luther King assassination, the civil rights movement. I was six during the missile crisis. I've got a photographic memory, so I remember these events.

The first activist thing I did, though, was in 1971. I circulated a petition at my suburban Montreal high school, demanding that the American Government, which was Richard Nixon then, stop doing nuclear testing in Alaska and Amchitka. Some of my friends made fun of me and said, "Hey man, you should be hanging out with girls instead of getting involved in this stuff."

I believe in reincarnation, and I think in every life you have a theme. I think, in this one, we're there when we are needed. We're here, in this life, to help people. We're not CEOs, we're not rich, we don't drive BMWs, but we've achieved things. We've had some successes. Twenty years ago we saved the Calvington bus route. We went door to door for three months, every house, and we personally got most of the thousand signatures. What two people can do if you believe in something! The bus route is still there.

B: The North York municipal building is still there. We were also part of the fight against the Front Street extension. After I graduated from the Community

Worker program at George Brown College, I fought to get free computers available there for alumni who needed them. At first we got a few old dinosaur computers – it took a lot of blood, sweat, and tears, but we got the same level of computers as everyone else.

K: In 1990 when former Metro Chairman Alan Tonks was prepared to cut funding to Meals on Wheels, I went to the committee and reminded them that seniors need those meals, and that the program provides jobs. They backed off.

In 1999 I also helped to get a regulation changed at the food banks. There used to be a lot of junk donated – like chips, cookies, and food that was out of date. After I got sick and was hospitalized from bad food at the food banks, I worked to convince them to pass a regulation to prevent companies from donating expired food. You know, my father used to tell me, "Whatever you do in life, do it well." Well, I listened.

A critical issue for us, that frustrates me, is that we are probably the most misunderstood. A lot of people don't understand us because we don't operate the way they do. I want to be understood, listened to, accepted.

B: We have to fight all the time to be recognized, respected, heard. Like, I have to fight to be able to say something in a meeting. That happens a lot.

K: I think it's about discrimination. People look at us and figure, "Hey, these people look stupid," and they talk down to us. People can know us for so long, and still not really know us. When we have social events with activists they often only talk about their work. I have a wickedly funny sense of humour, combined with a gift for mimicry for voices [think Rich Little here – Cathy], but activists never get to see that side of me, not even at the Imperial Pub. I have to be very, very serious because everyone else is always serious. One flaw we have as activists is we don't realize there are more dimensions to people, and don't allow ourselves to explore that.

ON THE SOLUTION: HOUSING

K: I'm interested in solutions. Sixty years ago, after World War II, we had a housing shortage. Men returned from Europe and the Pacific, and there was a

We Remember Them

We remember them,

We remember when.

They danced with joy of life,

They cried with occasional strife.

They shared with us their future plans

We felt the love in their strong hands.

They played jokes and made us laugh,

Until we thought we'd split in half.

They shared the wisdom of their years,

Told us their pleasures and their fears.

They had jobs and made good money,

Everything for them looked sunny.

They had families, wives and kids,

Until their lives hit the skids.

They never thought that they would be

Spending their time on the street.

Their lives collapsed, their worlds caved in.

They would never go back to where they'd been.

Suddenly, their world was changed,

Their whole reality rearranged.

They died homeless. Does society care?

They probably didn't even know they were there.

That is why we remember them.

We want society to remember when.

– Bonnie Briggs

housing crisis. There was public support then to do it. In the '70s, same thing, and that's what we need now. We need the public will again. I want Ottawa to wake up and assume, fulfill, their responsibilities, for all Canadians.

B: The government must get back into housing. They took us out, they can put us back into it.

For me, it's about breaking the stereotypes around homelessness. We can't leave people there.

Do people choose to sleep outside? People aren't out there because they want to be. It's not their fault. We didn't choose to be homeless, and we were out there.

Why can't they go into a shelter? Number 1: they're overcrowded. Number 2: they're full of infections like TB and bedbugs. They're not that safe, and to be honest, they're not that clean, and they're not meant for people to live in for fourteen years!

Why can't they get a job? What jobs! If you're on the street you can't get the clothes you need for an interview. There's no way an employer can get hold of you. How can you run all over town for interviews, and even get a good sleep at night to be fresh in the morning?

Whenever people talk about the status of homelessness, or the conditions of shelters, it's always about singles and families with children. They don't talk about couples that don't have kids – like us.

K: That good old British work ethic – "Oh, everybody should have a job." Well, last time everyone seemingly had a job was during the Second World War. That was the last time we had full employment. Full employment is a myth.

ON LIFE AND THE FUTURE

K: We were homeless. When we came off the street we made a vow – "never again." We are able to keep going because we look after each other and our cats. And the work needs us.

B: We got internet, phone, and cable this week. We waited eleven years to be able to afford them.

K: The last time we had a phone was fifteen years ago. We know a lot more people now. I think a lot of people will call us. "Thank you, Mike Harris" – we've had ten years of not being able to afford necessities – like a phone, like the internet, which for us is a necessity.

It's like a trade-off. We haven't been rich, but well, we've been in a movie, we've been in a play, we've written a book, and I host a radio show. Honestly, we get to do things that other people only dream of.

B: In five years, I hope we won't be renting anymore and we'll share a place, like a townhouse or a condo. Maybe with a friend. We'll still be in the city because I need to be close to stores and transit, and close to my work and friends. I hope we'll still be healthy and that our cats will be healthy. We might even have a dog by then.

K: I have an even closer goal. My youngest brother never hit forty and my father died three months short of turning fifty. I'm coming up on the front fifty, and now I'm getting to work on the back fifty. I want to make my fiftieth birthday, and then I want to live until I'm a hundred, even though I do have some physical disabilities.

I hope that I'll be in a saner, less stressful place in five years. We've survived the last ten years of stress. I think, not only for us, but for a lot of people, especially in Ontario, these years have been really stressful. More people suffered under the Mike Harris/Ernie Eves government, and now there is a big backlog of problems to fix.

I have what I call anchors, things that keep me going. I have emotional anchors, things that I care a lot about – like the City of Toronto Archives. That history means something. We all need emotional anchors to survive. We're hopeful for our future.

MELVIN TIPPING decided, after more than twenty-five years, to search for his family. He reconnected with two sisters who were still living in Winnipeg. He began a correspondence with one sister, Doreen, to whom he wrote: "I hope to see you alive and happy before I go up to heaven. This picture shows my age but it doesn't show how good-looking I am. I only have a beard because it shows my sympathy for the homeless." Melvin continued to consider Evangel Hall his community, and to attend programs like the men's group on a regular basis. In December 2006 he spoke once again at the Homeless Memorial, which now recorded more than five hundred names. In the ensuing weeks his health rapidly deteriorated, and he died. Melvin was both stubborn, and extremely committed to homeless people's needs – even in the final years of his life. Even though he liked and respected her, for several years he had refused to see his family doctor from the local community health centre. He was angry. He had resigned from the centre's board, incensed at their refusal to use the lower level of their building for an Out of the Cold program. To date there is no emergency shelter or Out of the Cold in Parkdale, the neighbourhood Melvin called home for more than fourteen years.

DRI is still living in the same home he moved into after the Tent City eviction. He has taken great joy in spending time with his mom and two teenagers. He visits them often in Waterloo. They recently came to hear him lecture at Sir Wilfred Laurier University in Waterloo. Dri remains active with the Toronto Disaster Relief Committee.

NANCY BAKER became homeless again for several months, but moved back into housing thanks to the Tent City program. Her prediction that the City of Toronto's homeless count would miss people, proved accurate. Nancy continues to speak out, in particular about the city's mean-spirited practice of not allowing agencies to provide life-saving supplies, like food and sleeping bags, to people who are forced to live outside.

MARTY LANG is still part of what is affectionately called the "program" – the Tent City emergency housing program. He remains connected with many organizations and remains a thoughtful, wise, and eloquent spokesperson.

BRIAN BOYD's picture still hangs in the All Saints drop-in. His dog Chaos is loved and cared for by friends Randy and the Colonel, and Chaos has gained a lot of weight. I have no doubt that if Brian were alive today he would be one of our main campaigners for a national housing program.

THE COLONEL continues to speak to media, and proudly attends rallies and demonstrations. He has remained brave, speaking the truth during a period when many social service organizations have withdrawn from advocacy. He too remains in his housing.

JAMES KAGOSHIMA would be disturbed to see how other Canadian municipalities have followed Toronto's lead – endless and repeated counts of the homeless, passing and enforcement of laws against them, evictions of people from outdoor sleeping spots, and reliance on the charitable sector instead of adequately funded and staffed services. He would undoubtedly join the housing activists who gather each month outside the Moss Park Armoury, and join their call for the downtown building to be converted into social housing, and no longer be used as a training place for war.

KEVIN CLARKE was not successful in his bid to represent Ward 20 on Toronto's City Council. He subsequently ran for mayor, in 2006, against David Miller and Jane Pitfield, and received more than two thousand votes.

During his mayoralty campaign he persistently raised housing issues. He was arrested at least once for boisterous campaigning, and was incarcerated in a hospital against his will. Several of his friends and advocates forced the hospital to release him. Although Kevin still campaigns periodically from the sidewalks, he is happy to have a home in Parkdale.

BONNIE BRIGGS and **KERRE BRIGGS**: Bonnie was finally approved for her disability benefits. The Homeless Memorial, that Bonnie helped create, won the *NOW Magazine* Best Memorial award in 2005. Kerre had a near-fatal heart attack in early March 2006, and is taking a very necessary time-out from activism to look after his own health. The pair continue to live in Parkdale, with their cats. They pursue their many interests, including music, photography, and writing.

□ □ □

These remarkable individuals have spoken and they have acted. Some have died.

Homelessness needs to be everyone's struggle today because there is still no national housing program. Homelessness, or being "dehoused," is what is downwind from poverty. It is what is downwind for ordinary people, from St. John's to Halifax to Montreal, to Gatineau, to Ottawa, to Kingston, to Belleville, to Cobourg, to Peterborough, to Oshawa, to York Region, to Toronto, to Guelph, to Hamilton, to Windsor, to Sarnia-Lambton, to London, to Sudbury, to Thunder Bay, to Kenora, to Winnipeg, to Saskatoon, to Edmonton, to Vancouver, to Victoria. These are places where I have visited, where I have seen it.

The expression "The Wind that Shakes the Barley" originates from an eighteenth-century Irish ballad by Robert Dwyer Joyce. Irish rebels carried grains of barley in their pockets as provisions. Slain rebels were often buried in mass, unmarked graves, called "croppy holes." From the pockets of the dead the grains would sprout and grow, thereby marking the croppy holes with stands of barley. So barley came to symbolize death under oppression, as well as resistance and regeneration.

We need a *wind* to make things happen, a *wind* that will lead to the mobilization of people for social change. A *wind* that will stir people, energize and warm people, and compel people to gather, to be vocal, to insist on and to fight for what is right.

In the past the *wind* has led to abolition, suffrage, and the defeat of Nazism; to reproductive rights; to the end to British colonial rule; to the overthrow of terrible dictatorships in developing countries like Cuba and Nicaragua; to the end to the Vietnam War; to the end to apartheid in South Africa; to human rights – almost world-wide acceptance that racism is wrong, that homophobia is wrong; and closer to home, to economic rights – the right to organize trade unions, to a shorter work week, to a minimum wage, to social insurance, welfare, health care.

But there has not been a wind to ensure the right to housing – at least not yet. We need a fully funded, national housing program for everyone, so that no one in this country remains homeless.

People are still dying for a home. We need a wind.

– Cathy Crowe

I THINK EVERYONE WHO HAS A VOICE IN THIS BOOK WOULD WISH, as I do, that you will be angry that our governments are not working together to fund the right to safe and truly affordable housing. Your anger is vital to the momentum needed to create the wind for social change.

Here are some strategies and some resources that may be useful to you, your colleagues, and your family and friends, as we all fight to ensure this very basic human right – the right to a home.

- ☐ Stay informed. Check out some of the resources listed below, to learn more. Join an electronic mailing list to stay abreast of the issues, receive event notices, and find opportunities to take part in action on homelessness.
- ☐ Participate. Join a campaign and become a member of one of the organizations that work for social justice (information about campaigns is often found on their web sites).
- ☐ Communicate. Express your concern by writing letters to the editor, or phoning call-in shows.
- ☐ Tell your politicians. Ask every level of government what they are doing about homelessness and the housing shortage in your community. Arrange to meet as a group with a politician who represents your area.
- ☐ Donate/fundraise. Making a financial contribution, to an advocacy organization in particular, goes a long way towards influencing public policy. Use a community event as a fundraising benefit for an organization that works on homelessness and/or housing.
- ☐ Get involved. Connect with others who might be interested in this issue – your friends, family, a social group, or people in your place

of worship, your neighbourhood, or your workplace. Do something concrete, like holding a screening of a film about housing or homelessness for your book club, your staff meeting, or your social network.

Here is a range of resources that may be helpful. In addition to these, there are numerous local anti-poverty groups and organizations working to build social housing.

ORGANIZATIONS AND ONLINE RESOURCES

Canadian Centre for
Policy Alternatives
www.policyalternatives.ca
(613) 563-1341

The CCPA is an independent, non-partisan, institute concerned with issues of social and economic justice. Their research and analysis show that there are workable solutions to the policy questions, including homelessness, facing Canadians today.

□

Canadian Housing and Renewal
Association (CHRA)
www.chra-achru.ca
(613) 594-3007

Established in 1968, the Canadian Housing and Renewal Association is a national, non-profit organization dedicated to supporting and strengthening the social housing sector.

Campaign 2000
www.campaign2000.ca
(416) 595-9230

Campaign 2000 is a cross-Canada public education movement aimed at building Canadian awareness and support for the 1989 all-party House of Commons resolution to end child poverty in Canada by the year 2000.

□

Cathy Crowe's website
and e-newsletter
www.tdrc.net/CathyCrowe.htm

Resources and a monthly electronic newsletter on pertinent and emerging issues related to health and homelessness, and the campaign for a national housing program.

Centre for Equality Rights in Accommodation (CERA)
www.equalityrights.org/cera
(800) 263-1139

CERA is a non-profit human rights organization that promotes human rights in housing. CERA works to remove the barriers that keep disadvantaged individuals and families from gaining access to, and retaining, the housing they need.

□

Co-operative Housing Federation of Canada
www.chfc.ca
(800) 465-2752

The Co-operative Housing Federation of Canada (CHF Canada) is the organized voice of the Canadian co-operative housing movement, working actively for the growth, stability, and independence of the movement in Canada.

□

FRAPRU
www.frapru.qc.ca
(514) 522-1010

Le FRAPRU est un regroupement national de lutte pour le droit au logement. Avec cent dix groupes membres dans les différentes régions du Québec, le FRAPRU lutte priori-

tairement pour le développement de nouveaux logements sociaux: habitations à loyer modique, coopératives d'habitation, et autres logements sans but lucratif.

□

Housing Again
www.housingagain.web.ca

A site dedicated to putting affordable housing back on the public agenda.

□

HomeComing
www.homecomingcoalition.ca

HomeComing Community Choice Coalition promotes the rights of people with mental illness, who face the most acute discrimination, to live where they choose. Their goal is to ensure that no one is stopped from living where they want to because of "Not-In-My-Back-Yard" discrimination.

□

Make Poverty History
www.makepovertyhistory.ca

A campaign with over 230,000 signatories calling for more and better aid, trade justice, debt cancellation, and an end to child poverty in Canada.

*National Aboriginal
Housing Association*
www.aboriginalhousing.org
(613) 258-6889

A membership-based organization, NAHA represents the interests of non-reserve Aboriginal housing providers in cities, towns, and the north.

□

*National Anti-Poverty
Organization*
www.napo-onap.ca
(613) 789-0096

The National Anti-Poverty Organization (NAPO) is a non-profit, non-partisan organization that represents the interests of low-income people in Canada.

□

*National Coalition on
Housing and Homelessness*
www.housingnow.ca

The Coalition believes it is time for the federal government to take action to deliver housing that low-income Canadians can truly afford. They support a new, dedicated, federal social housing program to help build 25,000 family and individual homes per year, for at least the next decade.

*National Homelessness Initiative
(Federal Government)*
www.homelessness.gc.ca

The National Homelessness Initiative (NHI) assists governments and community organizations to come together to alleviate homelessness.

□

*National Working Group
on Women and Housing*
www.equalityrights.org/NWG
(800) 263-1139

With representatives from every province and territory, the National Working Group on Women and Housing (NWG) has been working since 2003 to put women's housing and homelessness issues on political, legal, and policy agendas across Canada. Using a human rights framework, they advocate for policies and programs that will improve women's access to housing that is safe, secure, stable, and affordable.

□

Raising the Roof
www.raisingtheroof.org
(416) 481-1838

Raising the Roof is Canada's only national charity dedicated to long-term solutions to homelessness.

Toronto Disaster Relief Committee / National Housing and Homelessness Network
www.tdrc.net
(416) 599-TDRC (8372)

TDRC advocates on housing and homelessness issues. It was TDRC that declared homelessness a national disaster and demanded that Canada end homelessness by implementing a fully-funded National Housing Program through the "1 percent Solution." TDRC is the co-ordinating body for the National Housing and Homelessness Network.

BOOKS

Hulchanski, D., and Shapcott, M., eds. *Finding Room: Policy Options for a Canadian Rental Housing Strategy.* Toronto: University of Toronto Press, 2004.

Hurtig, M. *Pay the Rent or Feed the Kids?* Toronto: McClelland and Stewart, 2000.

Interfaith Social Assistance Reform Coalition/MacAdam, M., ed. *Lives in the Balance: Ontario's Social Audit.* Kitchener: Pandora Press, 2004. [Includes a chapter entitled "Nowhere to Call Home: The Housing Crisis," written by Michael Shapcott. A new edition is expected in spring 2007.]

Layton, J. *Homelessness: The Making and Unmaking of a Crisis.* Toronto: Penguin Books, 2000. [A new edition is anticipated in spring 2007. Working title: *Still Homeless!*]

Lorinc, J. *The New City.* Toronto: Penguin Books, 2006.

May, E. *How to Save the World In Your Spare Time.* Toronto: Key Porter Books, 2006.

Raphael, D., ed. *Social Determinants of Health: Canadian Perspectives.* Toronto: Canadian Scholars Press, 2004.

Sewell, J. *Houses and Homes: Housing for Canadians.* Halifax: James Lorimer and Company, 1994.

Swanson, J. *Poor-Bashing.* Toronto: Between the Lines, 2001.

FILMS

Fighting Words: The Social Crusades of Joseph E. Atkinson. 2006. Canada: Atkinson Charitable Foundation. (available from <www.atkinson.foundation.ca>)

Connolly, M. 2003. *Shelter From the Storm.* Canada: Brink Inc. (information at <www.tdrc.net>)

Saywell, S. 2002. *Street Nurse.* Canada: Bishari Film Productions Inc. (information at <www.tdrc.net>)

There are many other films addressing poverty and homelessness, that are useful tools for discussion. For example, *The Grapes of Wrath, Salt of the Earth, Fort Washington,* and *The Pursuit of Happyness.*

ACKNOWLEDGEMENTS

PAUL EPRILE WAS THE FIRST PERSON TO PLANT THE SEED, WHEN many years ago he urged me to write a book. That seed came to fruition when Between the Lines agreed to publish *Dying for a Home*. It has been an honour to work with Paul, David Glover, and Jenn Tiberio at Between the Lines, because of their talents, and their commitment to social justice. David Vereschagin's design has imparted beauty to this deserving material.

This book would not have come to life if Morris Wolfe had not introduced me to the work of Studs Terkel, James Agee, and Walker Evans, and convinced me that I could provide a contribution that would honour homeless activists in Canada. Morris not only came up with the concept of allowing homeless activists' voices to be heard, but he also gently walked me through the early stages of the process. From the bottom of my heart, I also thank each participant in the book for entrusting me with their life stories, when so often their voices have been misrepresented or ignored.

Catherine Dunphy introduced me to Daphne Hart (of the Helen Heller Agency), who became my literary agent, and skilfully guided me through this new and scary experience. Meg Taylor carried out an early edit, and demonstrated how to honour these expert voices. Linda Johnson also provided crucial editing advice. Rick Archbold gave this book its bloom.

A special thanks to Michael Connolly, who provided me with documentary film footage that allowed me to include the real voice of Brian Boyd. David Barker Maltby's family was extremely generous with the use of David's photos, making a number of these activists feel that their friend was still part of their struggle. Many talented people helped transcribe hours of valuable tape: Morris Wolfe, Lisa Ayuso, Tanyss Obonsawin, Rebecca Greenberg, and Sara Cohen.

Gratitude and love to Laura Sky, who told me: "You have to go to the Blue Mountain Centre!" She knew only too well that I needed to get away, and be left alone, to write. To my surprise, the Blue Mountain Centre, dedicated to social change, accepted me for a month-long residency program as a writer. There, surrounded by the natural beauty of the Adirondacks, nourished by an amazing kitchen, and stimulated by the companionship of staff and residents, I wrote! Special appreciation to co-residents Norma Smith, for our hikes and talks about equity, justice, and life, and Richard Claude, a renowned author on human rights, who, having read the chapter on James, wrote: "Human rights are about human beings, and James Kagoshima was an unforgettable and beautiful human being." His words validated this project and its purpose.

While working on this book I was also involved non-stop with the worsening homeless situation, and the further withdrawal of government funding. Bob Crocker and Dave Meslin (Mez) provided endless exuberance, creative energy, and talent, in support of that ongoing work. Family, and my "normal" friends (you know who you are), provided love, support, and many opportunities for meals and movies in between all the crises.

Both Beric German and Michael Shapcott have remained my dear friends for close to twenty years of this fight. I am deeply indebted to their teachings and leadership.

In 2004 I was given an opportunity for which I continue to feel very thankful. Charles Pascal, Executive Director of the Atkinson Charitable Foundation, and Betsy Atkinson Murray, Chair and President of the Board, asked me in to meet with them. They informed me that I would be the recipient of the Atkinson Economic Justice Award for three years. They gave me what they refer to as a "tap on the shoulder," and the support to "do what I do," which is to work on one of the most basic health and human rights issues – the right to housing. In early 2007 the Foundation announced an extension of my fellowship. Thanks to Board members and the staff – Charles Pascal, Christine

Avery-Nuñez, Pedro Barata, Elizabeth Chan, and Lynne Slotek, for helping to make my work possible.

Home is important in many ways, and I could not have worked on this project had I not had a respecting and safe workplace during my fellowship. Suzanne Boggild and the staff at the Sherbourne Health Centre welcomed me with open arms into their organization, amidst their own rapid growth and new building development.

And finally, I thank the Toronto Disaster Relief Committee, a very special organization. At its heart are some men and women who saw first-hand, and understood, that the devastation of homelessness went beyond Toronto's borders, and was national in scope. They had the courage to declare homelessness a national disaster, and to make the nation stand up and take notice.

– Cathy Crowe, Toronto, 2007

IMAGE CREDITS